Opening Minds

A Parents' Guide to Teaching for Thinking at Home

Selma Wassermann

ROWMAN & LITTLEFIELD

Lanham • Boulder • New York • London

Published by Rowman & Littlefield
An imprint of The Rowman & Littlefield Publishing Group, Inc.
4501 Forbes Boulevard, Suite 200, Lanham, Maryland 20706
www.rowman.com

86-90 Paul Street, London EC2A 4NE, United Kingdom

British Library Cataloguing in Publication Information Available

Library of Congress Cataloging-in-Publication Data

Library of Congress Control Number: 2020951169
ISBN 978-1-4758-5953-9 (cloth : alk. paper)
ISBN 978-1-5381-9117-0 (pbk : alk. paper)
ISBN 978-1-4758-5954-6 (electronic)

Dedication: This one is for Ruben who has his hands around my heart and for the adorable Maya who gave me such good help with the activities.

Contents

Preface

The idea for this book came during one of the darkest periods of our modern times. The COVID-19 pandemic that has taken many lives and caused intolerable suffering all over the world sent people into self-quarantine, shuttered nonessential stores, shops and offices, closed recreational facilities, schools, and libraries, tanking our formerly robust economy into a new recession. Small business collapsed, and large ones went bankrupt or ran billion-dollar deficits. Understandably people became more than anxious, not only about becoming ill, but about where we would all be when the worst of the spread of the disease was over.

We lived in self-imposed isolation in order to prevent the disease from further spreading. Face masks became mandatory in certain venues. Families who were accustomed to frequent social gatherings, now connected virtually with ZOOM, a far cry from feeling the embrace of our loved ones. Many parents became their children's teachers when schools were forced to close. At many colleges and universities, distance learning replaced lecture halls and seminars.

Watching from the window of the study where I write, I saw signs in windows of neighbors encouraging people to "hang in" because "we are in it together." Keeping two meters apart on park walks, I saw people maintaining that distance and cheerfully giving a V sign as acknowledgment of their thoughtfulness. I saw people in face masks in the market, waiting without complaint for their turn to enter, so that the store never became so overcrowded that it would be impossible to keep apart.

Yet, reading stories about other places, other venues, and other communities, I found that groups were banding together to voice protests against the restrictions that were put in place to protect us. Their arguments about the infringement of "their civil liberties" sounded mean-spirited; does "liberty" mean being free to spread infection? Drive-by protestors mocked and vilified people they saw in face masks—suggesting that the restrictions were a sign of some nefarious plot.

Upon reflection there seemed to be a huge disconnect between those people who were able to use the data to inform themselves about the intelligent actions we could take to move out of the dark period and those who were on the other side of the divide—those who ignored the data, who eschewed science, whose voices were loud in their unreasonable and unreasoned complaints and assertions, without the slightest nod to the data that should have informed their actions.

Those of us "in the know" understand and believe that good science informs us; that good data allow us to make better choices and intelligent thinking gives us the edge in our problem-solving capabilities. Those who live on the dark side, who protest without due cause, who see evidence of malice behind efforts to help and protect, seem to be lacking in some essential tools of rational mindedness. As far as being "critical thinkers" they seem to have been left far behind.

That awareness set in motion the burgeoning of ideas for this new book.

For if schools were to continue to be closed, or in some major way reduced in what they could reasonably offer children in the time to come, could parents become teacher-surrogates in implementing the very essential work of continuing to open children's minds so that they became more thoughtful, more rational in their choices, and more likely to use data to inform their actions? Would parents be sufficiently skilled to do this more sophisticated kind of teaching?

These are, of course, stilly questions because there is no doubt that parents are a child's first and ever-present teachers. From parents we learn not only to sing our ABC's, but also to "number" and to rhyme and to appreciate literature from the stories we are read to every night at bedtime. From parents we learn certain behaviors that make us more human, for example, to play fair, to share, to not hit our brother when he is bugging us, to clean up our room, to wash our hands before eating, and of course, to put the lid down on the toilet and flush. From parents we learn our values—and they guide our behaviors even before we understand the reasons for them.

Parents have been and continue to be our best teachers. Given that, it is not too far a reach to offer parents materials, resources, and the suggestions for the "how-to" that would enable and enhance children's intelligent habits of thinking, providing them with the "cognitive equipment" that would empower them to face any new situation, in classrooms, on the schoolyard, in the playground, at home, and in life.

It has been my joy, as a teacher, to have been able to share, with parents, their wishes, hopes, dreams, anxieties, and expectations for their children. Many of them have aided and abetted the work I did in classrooms, for the ultimate good of the children. I remember them with affection and regard and know, in my heart, that what I am offering here is not beyond their expertise or their ability. It is to that end that the ideas and activities in the following pages are presented, humbly, and with the sense that we teachers and parents are in a partnership to benefit the children in our charge.

Introduction

Talking to Parents

Eddie M. was one of a group of students who were invited to talk to pre-service teachers about his sixth-grade experiences as part of a "teaching for thinking" field research, and how that work benefited him as he embarked on his junior high school year. When asked by one of the adults how he managed the more rigorous demands of Grade 7 work as compared to the more open classroom experiences in Grade 6, he responded, without missing a beat: "We're such independent thinkers and problem solvers, we can handle any new situation."

Learning to think intelligently, like learning to derive meaning from the written word, requires experience and practice. Parents who want their children to become fluent in reading provide, in after-school hours, many opportunities for children to be read to, to go to the library, and to find books that they love. Moreover, these parents spend time with children in ways that further their reading skills, like teaching the letters of the alphabet, identifying rhyming words, and discussing parts of books that have particular appeal.

In the same vein, if intelligent habits of thinking are to flourish, children must have many opportunities to experience thinking at the higher cognitive levels of mental functioning. It is a huge error to believe that the development of intelligent habits of mind is a by-product of learning to read, to do math sums, or to give the right answers to test questions. Like other skills, the development of our cognitive powers requires concentrated and extensive work on those skills. As parents would contribute to improving children's reading abilities, so they might consider aiding and abetting what teachers do in classrooms to further children's intelligent habits of mind.

This parents' guide offers several hundred activities that engage children's cognitive abilities. As well it includes examples of the kind of parent-child interactions that contribute to the promotion of thinking at the higher cognitive levels.

LEVELS OF THINKING

An examination of what is meant by "thinking" is a good starting point. It is clear that thinking is a process that goes on in the mind during all of our waking hours (and perhaps during sleep as well). What's all the fuss about, then, if so much thinking is happening so much of the time?

Obviously, there is thinking and there is also "thinking." That is to say, thinking differs in kind, in intensity, and in outcome. When we try to remember the words of an old song, we are thinking. When a young man "dreams" of his beloved, he is thinking. When Lucy fantasizes about what she will wear to the senior prom next month, she is thinking. When mom and dad figure out their income tax returns, they are thinking. When Sara names the three ships of Columbus for her teacher, she is thinking.

When Paul uses the Pythagorean theorem to solve a math problem, he is thinking. When Mikhail Tal works out his next chess move, he is thinking. When Proust remembers his childhood through a bite of a madeleine cookie, he is thinking. When Stephen King conjures up a plot for his next thriller, he is thinking. When research scientists work to develop a vaccine for COVID-19, they are thinking. When the NASA group designed the "life on Mars" experiments, they were doing some thinking.

From these examples, it is easy to see that under the title "thinking," many different processes occur. It is also easy to see, from the examples, that these different acts of thinking differ in quality as well as in cognitive demands. We would not disagree that there is a considerable difference between the kind of thinking Lucy does as she decides on her prom outfit and the kind of thinking required in a championship chess match; or between the kind of thinking needed in recalling the names of the Pinta, Niña, and Santa Maria, and the thinking required in designing experiments to test for life on Mars.

Sometimes adjectives are attached to the word thinking to help explain the different cognitive demands. For example, there is "critical thinking," "productive thinking," "creative thinking," and "divergent thinking." These categories are generally considered to be on a higher cognitive level than the kind of thinking required in the recall of factual information

To be honest, it is very difficult to say, without an MRI, what actually occurs when the mind is engaged. We cannot tell from looking at a person's eyes or his or her facial expressions whether that person is doing some high-level cognitive exercise or whether that intense look is a sign of stress. We can, however, make a determination of the kind and quality of thinking when we examine the outcome. So far, outcomes and behavior give us the best clues as to what's going on "up there."

Some noted behavioral psychologists, like Benjamin Bloom (1956), and more recently, Kahneman (2011) have helped us to understand a little more about these differences in cognitive levels. Bloom gave us a taxonomy in which he identified different levels of thinking, for example, "lower cognitive" and "higher cognitive." Kahneman wrote about two systems of thinking that drive the way we solve problems and make choices: System One is fast, intuitive, and emotional. It doesn't take a lot of mental work. System Two is slower, more deliberative and more logical. It is harder and requires more mental effort.

Both Bloom and Kahneman, using different labels, are identifying similar processes—that is, how we distinguish those different levels of cognitive functioning. What Bloom also makes clear is that if a person can easily perform at the lower cognitive levels, those skills are not transferable to higher-level functioning.

That means that a child who can do well at remembering names, dates, and places may not be able to transfer that ability to designing experiments. In the view of many, the ability to design experiments is considered of higher value than the ability to recall information. It is also clear that the process of "designing experiments" occurs on a higher, more sophisticated level of cognitive ability than recalling information. From this it is possible to see that:

- there are differences in kind and in quality of thinking.
- children who function effectively on low level cognitive tasks cannot necessarily transfer those skills to succeed at higher level cognitive tasks.
- to become more proficient at higher level cognitive functioning requires experience and practice at these levels.

MATERIALS AND ACTIVITIES
THAT PROMOTE THINKING

Not all curriculum and homework tasks require higher-level thought. So, at the beginning, it is important for parents to know the difference between "activities" and "thinking activities." The latter term is being used to refer to those materials and tasks that engage children at the higher cognitive levels.

One of the essential differences between "thinking activities" and "activities" is that the former are inquiry oriented. The purpose of a thinking activity is to promote the process of inquiry. Most thinking activities are open ended, that is, they do not lead children to a specific answer or set of answers. Usually, many different responses are acceptable and appropriate in thinking activities.

Activities, on the other hand, generally lead to a specific answer; the goal of an activity is to help children arrive at the "right" answer.

For example, in a "thinking activity," children might be asked to develop hypotheses to explain why it had taken two weeks for an airmail letter mailed from Chicago to arrive in Los Angeles. In such a task, inquiry into several possible alternative explanations is the important feature of the activity. No single, correct answer is sought. An "activity" on the other hand, might require children to calculate the distance that a letter travels from Chicago to Los Angeles. Completing ten math problems, practicing spelling words, and selecting the "right" word to complete a sentence are examples of "activities." In "activities" children are expected to arrive at the correct answers. It is the answer, or the product, that is sought and rewarded.

In his book *Teaching for Thinking: Theory and Application* (1966), Louis Raths describes a dozen mental operations that require children to engage in thinking at higher cognitive levels. These operations provide a framework for the development of thinking activities for children. What's more, activities based in these operations may reflect subject matter in social studies, science, language arts, mathematics—in just about any subject area found in school. The following chapter and chapter 2, describes the thinking operations, which are the basis for generating the thinking activities presented in chapters 4 and 5.

CONCLUSION

This guidebook for parents explains, in greater detail, what "thinking activities" are; how they are different from "activities;" what the higher-order tasks demand cognitively; how parents may work with, or stand by, as children meet the cognitive demands; how parent-child interactions may work to suppress or facilitate further thinking; and what kinds of observable gains parents might expect to see in children as they grow in their cognitive skills. Several hundred examples are included that make higher-order cognitive demands and that cut across the main subject areas. The examples are categorized according to which are more appropriate for primary and which for intermediate students.

None of that is beyond the reach and expertise of parents.

Chapter 1

Opening Minds

What's the Big Idea?

Our teacher taught us about Henry VI who had 8 wives and beheaded them all. It was exciting.

Every parent wants their children to be of independent mind, self-directing, considerate, resourceful, thoughtful. Parents want their children to think before they act. When children face new situations, parents hope they will be able to apply their knowledge to solve new and hitherto unforeseen problems. Parents also hope that their children will be able to see through the propaganda, the disinformation, and the lies that make up so much of the social and political discourse of current times. Parents hope that their children will become capable adults who can take on the innumerable challenges of this twenty-first century.

Why on earth are these things so important? Perhaps it's because we believe that our very survival depends on being more rational, more thoughtful, and ready to take on the challenges of the future. Perhaps it's because we realize that we can't be both stupid and make our democracy work. Perhaps it's because we recognize that stupidity doesn't serve us well in dealing with the problems that face us not only today but in the future. Knowing the names of all the generals of the Civil War may give us a better mark on a test, but it is hardly helpful in tackling the demands of a problem never before seen or imagined.

Who would have thought that first world countries would succumb so easily to an infection that spread quickly throughout the land, killing thousands, laying waste to our strong economies, putting us into self-quarantine, locking up our favorite restaurants, libraries, schools, and recreational facilities. As we faced the fears, dangers, and the restrictions of self-isolation during the pandemic, those of us with the greatest resilience were able to rise to the occasion, find ways to cope, and to see the hard times through. Those with less cognitive equipment took to the streets and protested about the restrictions, with no regard for the health and safety of others.

Who knows what else lies in store for us in the future? And what skills, values, and attitudes will see us through and help us not only endure but overcome? Our long-term survival may depend on our collective ability to use our intelligent habits of mind to deal with what the future holds.

We will certainly need men and women with extraordinary skill, understanding, insight, and innovation to put our economies back on track. We will need that kind of expertise to ensure that we are never so unprepared to face another pandemic that might come our way. We will need men and women of superior talent to begin to address the massive destructive forces that are wrecking the planet. We will need men and women of considerable intellectual power to find ways to ensure better solutions to national enmities. These are only a few of the huge tasks that will claim serious attention as we recover, slowly but surely, from this current world crisis.

Which people will we put in charge of those seemingly insurmountable tasks? On whom can we count to help us not only to muddle through but to pull us out of the mire and onto safer land? Certainly not the test takers or the ones who know the correct names and dates. Certainly not those who see simple answers to complex problems. Certainly not anyone who leaps to conclusions before the data have been examined. Certainly not anyone who lacks sufficient analytic skills to dig into the belly of the problem and is afraid to try new ideas.

As we empower children to think for themselves, helping them to develop the skills to become more rational, more analytical, more confident in their abilities, more creative and inventive—they become our better angels. Our future is in their hands

Chapter 2

Getting Started

.

It may be tempting for parents who have nudged into this guide to bypass these introductory chapters and jump quickly into the chapters with the activities. But that would be a serious omission, for there are important advance organizers to the use of these "higher-order thinking tasks" that make them different from other curriculum activities. As well, they make different demands on the children.

But before that, parents may be reassured that what is being offered here has been tried and used successfully in classrooms across the globe. What's more, the evidence is strong that—used effectively—they do the job of expanding children's base of information as well as developing their critical thinking skills. In fact, it is safe to say that such tasks carried out over time will result in children becoming more thoughtful, more mature, more reflective, and more capable of solving problems and making sound decisions.

WHAT'S THE DIFFERENCE?

Unlike many homework assignments that ask children for the "right answers" these activities do not have right answers! This is a huge departure from the norm, and it may go against the grain for parents who have become habituated to urging their children to keep working to "get the answer." Right answers have been invested with much more than they are actually worth. If truth be told, they have been vastly overrated as vehicles that engage children's thinking on the higher-order cognitive scale.

So, one important difference is that thinking activities have no right answers. They may have better or less good responses, and encouraging children to think more about their responses is one means of promoting critical mindedness.

Another difference is that thinking activities begin with appreciation of "big ideas." Underlying this is the assumption that the content of each task, whether it is of observing, or comparing, or problem solving, will lead to deeper understanding of some central, significant issue, or issues. This is light years from a simple task that requires children to fill in blanks, color a pumpkin yellow, or add and subtract algorithms—tasks that children can do without having to suffer the pain of deeper thought.

A third difference is that there is no specified time limit for a thinking activity. Children may take as much time as each needs to think and come up with a personally satisfying response. Because critical thinking takes time, rushing through a task in a specified time limit does disservice to the nature of higher-order thought.

Finally, and equally important, is that thinking activities do not lend themselves to marking or grading. This includes the kinds of judgmental responses that indicate to the child that the parent agrees, or disagrees, or likes, or dislikes what the child has done. Yes, this may be discomfiting, certainly revolutionary. But these kinds of judgments and ratings are perhaps the most insidious and counterproductive ways that annihilate the most productive thought processes.

WHAT THE CHILDREN DO

At the very first, children need to understand the nature of the higher-order mental operation that is at the heart of each thinking activity. Each of these operations is described below. But it's a good idea for parents, before presenting a task to the child, to ensure that he or she understands what's required in the operation, that is, what is involved in comparing, or classifying, etc.

Pencil and paper may, of course, be used. A laptop, or tablet, if available, can also offer a way for children to put their ideas down. There is no one way that is advocated for all; whatever works, eh?

In the best of circumstances, children working with a partner or with a group of three serves several important purposes. First, they have an opportunity to discuss, to air ideas, to frame thoughts, before putting anything down on paper. This child-to-child interchange can be extremely productive. If there are siblings at home that can form such "study groups" it doesn't matter if there are age differences. Productive group discussions can be a valuable precursor to putting down one's ideas.

However, it may not be possible for home-based activities to enjoy the benefits of children working together. Never mind. Children working as individuals is better than not at all.

As children work through the thinking activities, they may raise questions to the parent, asking for clarification, or asking for specific help. In such cases, parents need to be forewarned NOT to do the child's thinking for him or her—but only to encourage, to clarify, and to support. The goal is NOT to get the answers, or to "get it right." The goal is to engage the child's thinking about the task he or she is doing.

THE ROLE OF THE PARENT:
CHOOSING THE ACTIVITY

Chapters 5 and 6 include hundreds of activities that engage children's thinking at higher cognitive levels. Each is based in a "thinking operation" (see chapter 3). The activities cut across several academic areas: math, language arts, social studies, and science. Art and creative writing are incorporated into a few of them.

Parents are free to choose a particular activity that seems "right" for the child's development level, for his or her interests, or for what, to the parent, seems important to study. Children should be invited to choose their own task. There is NO right order to doing the activities; they do not have to be done in sequence. In fact, there is no benefit in doing that. They may be chosen according to the above criteria, that is, interest, developmental level, what's important, or what may be connected to school studies.

Initially, the parent presents the task, making sure the child understands what the task requires and explaining why sharpening one's thinking skills is so important.

Then, the guidelines are presented:

- Do the best that you can do to figure it out for yourself.
- There are no right or wrong answers.
- There are no marks.
- I'll be around to help if you need it and to answer your questions.
- The most important goal is for you to do your best thinking.
- When you are finished, we can talk about what you have written.

Once the child begins work, the parent steps back so that the child may do his or her own thinking. Parents may encourage, support, answer direct questions (such as defining a word or clarifying the task), but should refrain from doing the child's thinking. Parents should also resist judging, praising, or rewarding what the child has done. Whatever responses the child makes on the task becomes "working material" for the parent in the post-task discussion.

Chapter 3

Thinking Operations

Those Higher-Order Mental Tasks That Engage Minds

The mental processes that are called "thinking operations" require children to put their minds to work. The operations ask them to do something more with information, something more than simply absorbing it from a page and recalling facts. This "more" involves more sophisticated and intelligent examination of that information and the suspension of judgment when the information is either lacking or not available. That kind of analysis leads to increased understanding of significant concepts or the "big ideas" of what is being studied.

In other words, learning to use the mental operations in examining information does not mean that information is unimportant. It does mean that children learn to use information more productively, rather than just storing it inertly for the purpose of recalling it at some later date.

It is of little benefit if a child remembers the dates during which World War I occurred. It is of greater benefit if a child understands the "bigger story"—for example, the background of why great countries were unable to resolve their differences without going to war, the participants, the nature of trench warfare, poison gas as a weapon, why the United States came so late to the table, the extent of casualties, and the results of the Treaty of Versailles. Thinking activities dig more deeply into the "big ideas" of the issue being examined, leading to greater understanding and appreciation.

The "thinking activities" included in chapters 5 and 6 are all rooted in one or more of the thinking operations described in this chapter.

But before moving on to those chapters, it's probably a good idea to begin with an understanding of what these mental operations are and how they function to serve the purpose, not only of promoting deeper understandings about the big ideas in the subject areas but also what they demand cognitively.

THINKING OPERATIONS: OBSERVING

When children are asked to observe, they make visual assessments of data. The data may appear in a graph, a text document, an image, or a cartoon. Observing may also involve listening, as well as touching, and smelling. In other words, observations permit us to collect data through a variety of senses.

When we ask children to observe we ask them to examine data with perceptiveness, with sharpness of mind, and with accuracy. We also ask them to report on their observations so that the accuracy of their observations may be assessed. When the children gain experience in making observations, they should have gained some skill in becoming more perceptive, as well as acquiring insight into what is being observed. This will help them understand a little more about the world in which they live.

An important criterion of a thinking activity that involves observing is that the task should present the child with something worth thinking about. For example, does this observation help the child to increase his or her understanding of the world? Will the task appeal to the child? Will it lead to new insights? Will it provoke further curiosity? These questions may serve as guidelines as parents choose observing activities for their children.

When children are more skillful in observing, they become more discriminating in the use of visual and auditory evidence and less inclined to accept the prejudices of others whose ideas are unsupported by evidence.

THINKING OPERATIONS: COMPARING

When children compare, we are asking them to look for similarities and differences. Sometimes, the two items being compared have a close relationship with each other, such as two animals, two musical instruments, or two books. Sometimes the items chosen for comparison have more subtle relationships, such as a tire and a submarine, a train and a caterpillar, and a marigold and a sea anemone.

For primary grade-level children, comparing animals, musical instruments, plants, machines, toys and a variety of items found in school and at home which are familiar in their lives is probably a good way to start. Older children may compare more complex items, such as the governments of two countries, two articles about the same subject from different newspapers, two characters in a play, or a contemporary and a classical work of art.

Comparing requires that children look for similarities as well as differences. As a result of many experiences in making comparisons students learn to observe more perceptively, and they learn to compare prior to drawing conclusions. As a result, they are more able to make better judgments and more informed choices.

Comparing activities should present children with materials that are worth thinking about, so that what is learned will lead them to acquire additional insights and awareness. When the content of a comparing activity is banal, or trivial, then the quality of the experience will inevitably be reduced.

THINKING OPERATIONS: CLASSIFYING

Being able to classify helps us to bring some order into our chaotic lives; it is a very helpful tool to use when we are feeling overwhelmed.

When we classify, we put things into related groups, and that is the important criterion for making classifications. In many cases, there are several ways to classify items, but the system chosen should have some purpose. Classification requires two steps: (1) the step of creating the categories and (2) the step of placing the item into the group.

In asking children to classify, they need to figure out their own categories; if we set the categories for them, we are taking away the opportunity for them to do the more demanding cognitive task.

Children should be well acquainted with the task of classifying, because they do a lot of it at home and in school. For example, we ask them to put the silverware away; knives, forks, and spoons are classified in the slots in which they belong. Underwear goes into this drawer and socks into that. In the kitchen cupboard, the dishes are stacked according to size and use; the foods onto separate shelves to make them easy to access as needed. The spice cabinet is classified alphabetically—since when we are reaching for turmeric, we don't have to sift through the entire collection.

From these simple kinds of groupings, we can see that being able to classify, to sort, and to organize data enables us to bring a bit more order into our lives.

THINKING OPERATIONS: IMAGINING

At first glance, you might not consider imagining one of the higher-order mental operations. That would be a mistake. For it is from imagination that great ideas surface, innovations occur, breakthroughs in art, music, and yes, even science come to the forefront of the mind. When children are asked to imagine, they let their minds wander to create those beautiful, fanciful, cotton candy worlds that the mind invents. At first, imagining may have no basis in reality. We ask children to create freely, to exercise that part of the mind that is frequently untapped in schoolwork.

Imagining gives rise to Rube Goldberg inventions, Dymaxion cars, Calder mobiles, cartoons, and films. From his imagination, Da Vinci created the diving suit, the aerial screw, the omithopter, and yes, the parachute. Revolutionary inventions that changed the word, such as the compass, the automobile, the steam engine, and the airplane came from the fertile imagination of the inventors of those earlier times. Not to mention the wheel.

Imagining may also bring humor, joy, spontaneity, and beauty into our lives, and children profit greatly from many opportunities to cultivate this rich inner resource. It would be hard to overestimate the value of unhampered imagination in confronting the problems of an uncertain future.

THINKING OPERATIONS: HYPOTHESIZING

This mental operation asks children to come up with a variety of possible explanations for a particular question, problem, or conundrum. It includes the process of identifying several alternative explanations, as well as the analysis of which of them have the most credibility. Older children may take this a step further by finding ways to test their hypotheses, a step that carries this operation to a higher level of difficulty.

Suggesting hypotheses is often seen in laboratory work as scientists come to grips with problems that as yet have no solutions. Looking for a vaccine for the COVID-19 virus means that scientists are hypothesizing potential avenues to pursue, as well as making determinations about which are more viable. But science labs are not the only sites where hypothesizing can be helpful. In human relations situations, we might hypothesize why a friend has not responded to our e-mail, why our dog is off his feed, why Amy is having trouble doing her math homework. When we face a problem, suggesting potential avenues of explanation prevents us from leaping to inane or faulty conclusions.

Developing skill in the mental operation of hypothesizing helps to free us from dogmatic assertions, from seeing life from only one perspective, and from "either/or" judgments. It is a skill that enables us to deal more effectively with the problems we face in our daily lives, as well as those that confront us in the wider community.

THINKING OPERATIONS: EVALUATING AND JUDGING

The higher-order mental operation of evaluating asks children to make judgments and offer opinions, in order to sharpen their ideas of what they consider desirable and undesirable, of high quality and inferior quality, of significant and trivial. In offering their judgments, children are asked to specify the criteria they have used in arriving at those judgments.

In these days of instant access to the media, to the Internet, to Tweets, Twitters, Facebook, and Instagram, criticism flows freely, without a second thought, without a care for the words being used, and without regard for the impact of the words on the recipient. It seems as if this new age of instant access to information gives license to anyone to voice an opinion, no matter how uninformed, how mean-spirited, how irrelevant to the actual big ideas of the message. As a consequence, people have been victimized unjustly, the cruelty of the comments leaving scars that endure.

It's easy to toss off a few harsh words of criticism, but much more difficult to consider not only the criteria on which the judgments are being formed but also with an eye toward how such judgments will contribute to the improvement of what is being judged.

Judgments that are informed, thoughtful, and responsible have, within them, the power to advance thinking. Judgments that are uninformed, thoughtless, or irresponsible have within them the power to harm. They serve no benefit other than to damage. As children learn to become more skillful using informed, thoughtful, responsible evaluative judgments, they develop a powerful tool for the improvement of the quality of our lives.

THINKING OPERATIONS: LOOKING
FOR ASSUMPTIONS

Assumptions are things we take for granted. We may take for granted something that is actually true. On the other hand, we may take something for granted that is probably true or probably false. In the higher-order mental operation of being able to identify assumptions, what is important is that children learn to recognize what assumptions are. That includes assumptions that they themselves make as well as assumptions made by others.

Learning to differentiate what is assumed to be true and what is observable fact is at the very heart of logical reasoning. When children acquire skill in their ability to recognize assumptions, they are less likely to fall prey to the seductive qualities of advertisers, of media merchants who spread disinformation, and of people who are conspiracy theorists. Children will be less inclined to accept propaganda as fact, experimental data as proof, and conclusions as "right." They will be less likely to leap to conclusions based upon limited evidence, less impulsive in their actions. How can such higher-order cognitive skills not be a considerable asset in the world in which we now live?

THINKING OPERATIONS: COLLECTING
AND ORGANIZING DATA

This operation is better left to the intermediate-level children as it may be too difficult for the primary graders. That is why thinking activities for this operation have not been included in chapter 5, for the younger child.

The ability to collect and organize information requires several skills. First, there is the skill of locating information, determining which are the appropriate references and the relevant sources. Then the sources need to be located. Second, there is the skill of examining the data, determining the accuracy and validity of the data, and selecting those portions that are relevant to the inquiry. A third skill involves the development of strategies that allow the data to be assembled.

Once the sources are identified and selected, the information is culled and gathered, the process of organizing the information can begin. Obviously, there are several ways to do this.

Data may be organized in stories, in essays, in graphs, in outlines, in bibliographies, in research proposals, in newspaper articles, in menus, and in personal dictionaries—to name but a few. Figuring out how to organize the data that have been collected in a systematic, logical, and coherent way and then doing the organizing is a complex process. But it is essential in sharpening children's abilities to locate and comprehend information.

A word must be added here about the selection of sources to gather information. Since much of our data gathering these days is from Internet sources and since so much of what is available on the Internet may be incorrect, or downright false, children need to be tuned in to methods of evaluating the truth of the information they have gathered. To help them understand the difference between information and disinformation is, perhaps, one of the more urgent higher-order cognitive skills of our time.

THINKING OPERATIONS: SUMMARIZING

The operation of summarizing requires the ability to condense, to distill from a piece of work its core message. To summarize, children must be able to state, briefly and coherently, the main ideas of something they have read, or seen, or heard, to be concise without missing the big ideas. They must also be able to differentiate between what is important and what may be left out.

This is another operation that may pose a greater challenge for primary age children—since many of them would rather elaborate than condense. Be that as it may, a few activities for primary graders have been included. If parents find them too far out of reach of their children, they can be delayed or even bypassed.

When children learn to summarize, they become better able to discriminate and discern relevant from irrelevant, significant from insignificant, and consequential from trivial, thereby increasing their understanding and cognitive power.

THINKING OPERATIONS: INTERPRETING

This is one of the more complex and demanding operations in the group of thinking operations. That may come as a surprise to many parents, but the data are clear that even graduate students working on doctoral theses have trouble making intelligent interpretations of the data from their research. That is one reason this operation has been excluded from the primary group of activities. It is also a reason that intermediate graders may have more difficulty than a surface examination of the task might suggest.

The mental operation of interpreting requires the ability to explain the meaning that an experience has for us. That is, "what is the essential message that can accurately be drawn from the experience or from a given body of data?"

When children are asked, "What meaning do you get out of this picture, this story, this event, this poem, etc.," they are being asked to interpret. When we interpret, we put meaning into and take meaning out of a body of data. We may interpret graphs, tables, charts, pictures, reports. We may interpret cartoons and jokes. We interpret poetry and prose, nuances of expression and body language.

Our ability to interpret accurately depends on how well we have "read" the message and on how skilled we are at finding the essence of what is being read or seen.

Where we go astray in interpreting is by missing the meaning—that is, drawing conclusions that are not supported by the data. We may also draw conclusions that go far afield from what the data allow. When children tell us, "I don't get it," they are telling us they have missed the meaning.

Gaining skill in the operation of interpreting enables children to derive more accurate meanings that add to the richness of living. Children who continually misinterpret and miss the meaning are severely handicapped in their ability to understand and derive satisfaction from their experiences. Learning how to interpret life's experiences is an important milestone along the road to maturity.

THINKING OPERATIONS: DESIGNING PROJECTS AND INVESTIGATIONS/PROBLEM SOLVING

While most of us solve problems and design investigations that occur daily, such as figuring out why the bread didn't rise, the car didn't start, the dog is off her feed, how to keep the crows off the bird feeder, or how to spend time productively during the self-imposed quarantine, there are problems and problems. Not all of them carry the same "weight." Not all of them are solvable. But all of them require careful analysis, clarity of the nature of the problem, and, of course, the development of strategies that are clearly connected to the solution of the problem.

Not the least is our ability to put a plan into action, and not to give up when the plan didn't work.

In order to make the operation of designing investigations/problem solving clear, it is helpful to understand that it includes several stages. First, one needs to be clear about the problem—that is, to define it in a way that will eventually lead to a plan. This may be more difficult than it sounds. Questions should not be confused with problem statements. Questions are more finite; problems have a larger scope.

Second, we must be able to determine what it is we need to know. For example, in the problem of the bread not rising, it would be important to know whether the yeast used is not past its expiry date, whether the time allotted for the rising was adequate, whether the place where the rise occurred was warm enough or too hot. Identifying what we need to know leads to the development of a plan.

Third, we must be able to suggest hypotheses about what has been observed to be the problem. Suggesting hypotheses leads to data gathering—checking on the expiry date of the yeast, checking the temperature of the rising site, checking the amount of time allotted for rising.

Gathering data from the investigations leads to the evaluation of the results. Which was the viable solution? Perhaps none of them? In that case, more hypothesizing and data gathering are needed.

Of course, not all of these sub-steps are necessary in the solution of every investigation; moreover, it will become clear, as one moves through the solution of different problems, that no single problem-solving method can be applied to all problems. To insist on such a single method (e.g., the "problem-solving method") for the solution of all problems would constrain rather than facilitate children's problem-solving abilities.

It may be fatuous to make a point of how important it is to develop a child's ability to design investigations and solve problems on his or her own. For younger children, well-meaning parents often remove the onus of solving problems from them. "Here, Marvin. Let me do that for you." We want to help. We want to make life easier for our beloved children. Yet in doing that, we remove from them the opportunity to work their minds, to figure things out, and to feel the satisfaction that solving a problem brings. We also remove from them the opportunity to face disappointment when a solution fails, learning to pick themselves up to try again.

Being able to feel confidence in solving problems on one's own is enabling. They are among the greater gifts that parents can give their children.

THINKING OPERATIONS: DECISION MAKING

Our lives are consumed with decisions that we make many times a day—from the more mundane, such as what to prepare for dinner, to the more complex, such as what methods could I have used to home school my kids during the self-imposed quarantine of the COVID-19 pandemic. It's true that more mundane decisions require less thought, less analysis, less angst in figuring out what to do. We may not even be aware that such activities require decisions to be made.

It's also true that more complex decisions require considerable thought, analysis, and reflection, more often leading to better decisions. When that process of informed reflection before making a choice is ignored or neglected, we may find ourselves trapped by a bad decision, one that has consequences that we later regret.

One reason that wrestling with difficult decisions seems "heavy" is because there are no "right answers" in our decision making. It's more a matter of which courses of action seem more reasonable and which actions are more in tune with what we believe to be right and good. In other words, "our decisions are us."

One of the purposes of including "decision making" in this set of thinking operations is to give children opportunities to examine the beliefs, attitudes, and feelings that lie behind the choices they make. In the event that children face several options, they will have a chance to determine, for themselves, what it is that really matters to them.

In these activities, children learn to examine the potential consequences of decisions they make, to themselves and to others. Having made their choices, children learn a little more about themselves, what kind of people they are, and what they stand for.

Why is that good? It seems clear that the ability to make thoughtful, judicious decisions in one's life, to be able to affirm the decisions one has made as "right and good," will undoubtedly add an important dimension to the quality of life. In the thinking process, as children learn more about what they believe to be right and what they believe to be wrong; what they care for deeply and what is unimportant to them; what they prize and what they scorn, they become more reasoned and reasonable adults, adults who are able to see the consequences of their choices and to accept responsibility for them.

It is not farfetched to conclude that the ability to choose wisely and thoughtfully is an essential component in promoting mature, responsible adulthood.

CONCLUSION

These are probably not the only mental operations that call for thinking at higher cognitive levels, but they are a strong start in providing a context in which activities can be generated that ask children to do more with information than simply store it. As mentioned earlier, this is not a revolutionary scheme to ignore the importance of information. It is rather a plea to use information in ways that inform, that bring the "big ideas" to light, to see what is relevant, what is absent, and what more we need to know to make an informed judgment.

The mental operations are the bedrock upon which the activities in the following chapters rest.

Chapter 4

Preparing

The activities in the next two chapters are divided into two groupings. Each group is based on the reading abilities of the children for whom the activities are intended. The first group of activities in chapter 5 has been constructed for children who cannot yet read or who are beginning to develop their reading skills. The second group, in chapter 6, is for those children who have gained fluency in reading.

It is important to note that not all operations cited in chapter 3 are included in the activities for pre- and emerging readers. As children gain in their maturity and their skill, they will be more able to deal with the operations that require those more sophisticated mental skills.

The tasks have been classified by operation, the activities encompassing several curriculum areas. Parents can select activities that are more likely to appeal to their children as well as those that are connected to school studies. Children may also make their own selections, which give them some control and agency over the development of their thinking skills.

SOME GROUND RULES

Before beginning, consider the following ground rules in opening the door to this homework:

- Explain to your child what you are asking of him or her and why you think this work is so important.
- Choose an activity in which the materials needed are easily available. Make sure you have the materials on hand before you begin.
- For children who are able to read, it's a good idea to present the activity on an index card or a piece of paper. This gives them a "hands on" piece of material to refer to as needed, as well as identifies the various aspects of the task.
- For pre- and emerging readers, you can take a more direct role, by presenting the task orally, describing what is to be done and how, and answering questions.
- As the child engages with the task, you should be available to answer questions, to encourage, to guide. Try to refrain from doing the child's thinking.
- After the child has completed the task, involve him or her in giving feedback on what has been done. That is, what did they like about it? What was too hard for them? What do they see as benefits of the work? Many examples of these child-parent discussions that plumb the mind and provoke further thought are included in chapters 5 and 6.
- Make observations about the way your child is working. Is the task too difficult? Does it cause frustration or anxiety? Does it seem too easy? Does the child dance through without adequate thought to the process? Use those observations to give your child the help he or she needs to tackle the next task more productively.

It is to be expected that most children may find the first few of the thinking activities new and different from other school work they have done. For that reason, it might take a few "trials" before the road ahead becomes smoother, and the children are better acquainted with the demands of higher-order thinking. In such cases, the parent is on hand to encourage, support, guide, and help as needed.

No child should feel that what he or she is doing is a task that is not worth their time. No child should feel anxious or unhappy about the work. No child should feel that he or she is not up to the task of doing his or her own thinking.

At the very least children should feel empowered by having gained skill in these thinking processes.

Chapter 5

Thinking Activities for
Pre- and Emerging Readers

There are several pre-conditions that parents need to be aware of in working with the pre-and emerging reader on tasks that call for higher order thinking.

First, parents will need to instruct children orally about the nature of the operation and what the activity requires.

Second, children will need to respond most of the tasks orally since they cannot be counted on, at this developmental stage, to record their work in written form. Not a problem! (Some ask for pictures to be drawn.)

Third, the parent will have to "stand by" with prompts as the child works through the task. This is done with careful and sensitive questioning. For example:

Parent: In this activity, you are being asked to compare a computer and a pencil. How are these alike? What can you tell me about them?
Child: You can use both of them to write.
Parent: That's one similarity. Can you think of some others?
Child: I can't think of any more.
Parent: How about differences? Can you think of the ways in which a pencil and a computer are different?

Child: You have to plug in your computer. But you can just use a pencil. It doesn't need electricity.
Parent: So one difference is that one needs electricity and the other doesn't.

Can you think of some other differences?

Child: You have to sharpen your pencil. Sometimes the point breaks. And you don't have to sharpen your computer. (Heh heh)
Parent: Pencils need to be sharpened. But computers just need to be plugged in.
Child: Yeh.
Parent: I see. How about other differences? Can you think of some more?

N.B. The sequence of mental operations, beginning with comparing, and leading to designing projects/problem solving, is a suggested way of proceeding, since the first three operations are more easily understood by young children and the latter four more challenging. This is, however, not writ in stone. Parents who know their children best should feel free to pick and choose among the operations which seem most promising for their child's thinking skills development.

Although the activities in each of the categories have been presented in an a to z sequence, there is no preferred "order" to doing them.

NOTES TO PARENTS FOR
COMPARING ACTIVITIES

A few activities require advance preparation. For example, if the child is going to compare two pictures cut from a magazine or newspaper, this will have to be done in advance of the task. If the child is going to compare two paintings, these will have to be selected in advance of the task. (Computer printouts of magazine or newspaper pictures and works of art are easily accessed.) Activities that require a bit of advance preparation are marked with an asterisk (*).

Pre-readers and emerging readers will need to respond orally, since asking for written responses would not be appropriate at this level.

Begin any comparing activity by explaining to the child what is called for in the operation; for example, comparing means finding the ways in which things are alike and finding ways in which they are different. Then present the activity and make sure the child understands what is to be done.

Children who choose to gather data from a laptop, a tablet, or any other data source should be free to do so. They should also be cautioned about the accuracy of the data gathered from the Internet. Wherever possible, the actual materials should be made available for children to observe, touch, and examine.

An Alphabet Soup of Things to Compare

What are some similarities? What are some differences?

a.   A bear and a pig
b.   A balloon and a kite
c.   Two pictures (cut from a magazine, a newspaper or a computer printout) *
d.   A fish and a turtle
e.   A dinosaur and a snake
f.   A computer and a pencil
g.   A cell phone and a tablet
h.   A flower (any flower) and a vegetable (any vegetable) *
i.   Christmas and Halloween
j.   A ruler and a measuring cup *
k.   Milk and ice cream
l.   Rain and snow
m.   A butterfly and a bird
n.   Mother's work and father's work
o.   A pair of scissors and a hammer *
p.   A pencil and a paintbrush
q.   An octopus and a goldfish*
r.   Pizza and hot dogs
s.   An eagle and an airplane
t.   An apartment house and a cabin
u.   Winter and summer
v.   A baby and a kitten
w.   The sun and the moon
x.   A rocket ship and a jet plane
y.   Air and water
z.   A square and a circle *

NOTES TO PARENTS FOR OBSERVING ACTIVITIES

It's a good idea to begin by making sure the child understands what he or she needs to do in the mental operation of observing. That is, observing means they are gathering accurate information about what they see (hear, touch, or smell). What is important in making observations is that they are true to what is seen and free from value judgments and assumptions.

In responding to the child's observations, checking for accuracy and for caution about assumptions and judgments can be made in a non-judgmental dialogue. For example:

Parent: Tell me about the observations you made about the weather.
Child: In the morning it was raining.
Parent: You made a picture of the weather in the morning and it was raining.
Child: Yeh. Then the next time I looked it was not raining any more. But I thought the sun would come out soon.
Parent: You saw something in the sky that told you it might get sunny later?
Child: No. I just guessed that it would come out. I just knew.
Parent: You made a guess? But you didn't see anything that told you that was true.
Child: I just made a guess. But I didn't know if it was true.
Parent: And what happened later? Was your guess right?
Child: No. When I looked later, it was raining again.
Parent: So what did that tell you about your guess?

An Alphabet Soup of Observing Activities

Activities that require some advance preparation are identified by an asterisk (*).

Ask your child to:

a. Make at least three observations of the weather during one day, at least one hour apart. Make some pictures of your observations of the weather.

b. Make some observations of clouds. What are some of the things you see? Try not to make any guesses; just tell what you observe.

c. Look at the video of the bears in the backyard pool (https://www. youtube.com/watch?v=77dtqOOaGLo). Tell what you have observed.

d. Cut out a picture of a person from a newspaper or magazine. Make some observations of that person. Try not to make any guesses.

e. You will need to ask your parent to keep the bones of a chicken or fish for you to study. * Then make some careful observations about what you see.

f. Find a picture from a newspaper, a magazine, or a book of a person doing some work. Make some observations of the work and the tools being used.

g. If there is a pet in the house, make some observations of the behavior of that pet over a two-hour time period.

h. Put a ruler on a ball and try to make it balance. Then tell from your observations how you made the ruler balance on the ball.

i. Put an onion (potato, a sweet potato, or other vegetable) in a dish of water. Watch the vegetable for a week and tell what you have observed.

j. Put a piece of bread in a dish in the sun. Watch the bread for a week and tell about the changes you have observed.*

k. Take a walk (with your mom or dad) around the block. When you return home, draw some pictures of what you have seen.*

l. Watch your mother or father preparing a meal or dessert and make some observations of what they did.

m. What do ice cream, apple, lettuce, bread, or pizza taste like? What observations can you make about the taste of these foods? The smell?

n. Touch several pieces of material, such as silk, velvet, burlap, and denim.* Make some observations about how they feel to the touch.

o. Listen to the sounds outside the window of your house or apartment. Are some sounds pleasant? Harsh? Soft? High? Low? Are there sounds that hurt your ears? What observations did you make about sounds?

p. Study some simple tools, like a pair of scissors, a screwdriver, a can opener, or a garlic press. Make some observations of how those tools work.*

q. Make a study of any musical instrument. * Make some observations about how musical sounds are made on it.

r.   You will need two buckets, one with some water and one empty. You will also need a rubber or plastic tube.* Then, use the tube to see how you can move the water from one bucket into the other. Make some observations about how that works.

s.   You will need a simple lever to do this activity. * (A 12" ruler can be used) How can you use the level to move something heavy? How does that work? What observations did you make?

t.   Make some observations about your best friend. How can you describe him or her? Try not to make any judgments or guesses in your observations.

u.   Try to remember an act of bullying that you have seen. Make some observations about what happened.

v.   Think of all the words you have heard that hurt someone's feelings. Ask your parent to make a list of them.

w.   You will need some ice cubes for this activity. * Put some in a dish, some in a glass, and some in a bowl. Put the dish, the glass, and the bowl with the ice cubes in different places in your house. Make some observations about the ice every ten minutes and tell what you have observed.

x.   What are some good ways to protect ourselves from germs and infection? What observations can you make about how we do that?

y.   Make some observations about what you see in a mirror.

z.   Make some observations about how you can tell how hot it is; how cold; how windy; how warm.

NOTES TO PARENTS ABOUT
CLASSIFYING ACTIVITIES

We classify objects to bring some order to our lives. We put our socks in one drawer and our underwear in another. We put the knives in one slot and the spoons in another. We put the toy cars in one box and the toy trucks in another. We put the puzzles on one shelf and books on another. That helps us to find what we need so that we don't have to go searching in a big heap of stuff.

Sonia bought a big box of books at a yard sale. When she got home, she classified them into four groups: one group was for the books she wanted to read. A second group was for the books that were too hard for her. A third group was for the books that were too easy for her. The last group was for the ones she wanted to donate to the book club. When Sonia classified her big box of books, that helped her to figure out what to do with them.

There are no right or wrong ways to classify; we put things into groups for some purpose. But our system of grouping should show that the groups have some relation to each other.

For pre-readers and emerging readers, the classifying activities may require a bit of advance preparation on the part of parents, since classifying tangible objects or pictures is a preferred way to begin.

An Alphabet Soup of Classifying Activities

a. Pictures cut from magazines that have some relation to each other
b. Story books
c. Crayons
d. Blocks
e. Toy cars
f. Foods
g. Jobs
h. Boats
i. Vehicles used for transportation
j. Animals (this may be further broken down into categories of each of the classes, such as birds, mammals, and reptiles)
k. Pets
l. Musical instruments
m. Toys
n. Buttons
o. Household tools (such as hammer, screwdriver, scissors, pliers, nails, level, ruler, etc.)
p. Writing tools (such as pencil, pen, tablet, laptop, paper, chalk, blackboard, index cards, and post-its)
q. Vegetables
r. Fruits
s. Letters of the alphabet
t. Relatives
u. Streets in the neighborhood
v. Fabrics

w.   Liquids
x.   Clothes
y.   TV programs
z.   Insects

NOTES TO PARENTS ABOUT
SUGGESTING HYPOTHESES

For the younger group of children who are not yet advanced in their reading skills, the word hypothesis itself may be a bit of a mouthful. But perhaps that is a good way to begin to introduce this thinking operation—by learning this new word and what it means.

For the Children: Hypotheses are special kinds of guesses. They can help you explain things that you don't understand.

For example, how do you suppose a spider learns to build a web? Here are some hypotheses.

Maybe a spider learns from watching other spiders. Is that possible?

Maybe a spider tries and tries to build a web until that spider gets it right. Is that possible?

Maybe a mother spider shows her spider children how to do it. Is that possible?

Maybe a spider already knows how to build a web when it is born. Is that possible?

Those are four hypotheses. They try to explain something that we don't know. They give us some ideas about how things work. But they are not answers. They are just possibilities. And some possibilities are more possible than others.

If you can think of good hypotheses they can help you to figure things out.

Here is how that works:

Kang has a rash on his face. What could be wrong?

Maybe he ate some peanuts and he's allergic to peanuts?

Maybe he touched poison ivy?

Maybe he is getting the measles?

Those are some hypotheses. They are trying to explain the reasons for the rash on Kang's face. A good hypothesis helps to lead you to the solution to a problem.

For the Parent: When your youngster is given a task in which he or she is asked to suggest hypotheses, at the very first, the child may just offer one possibility and then stop—as if the task was already completed. In that case, the following brief scenario may be helpful:

Parent: How come the ocean has so many waves? What hypotheses can you suggest to explain it?
Child: I don't know the answer.
Parent: Maybe you can think about some good guesses. Think about it for a minute. There are no right answers, just your best guesses.
Child: Okay. Let's see. Maybe it's because there was a big wind that made the waves.
Parent: Ah, so perhaps a big wind came and stirred up the water to make the waves.
Child: Yeh. It could be some big wind.
Parent: Perhaps you have some other guesses too?
Child: I don't know anymore.
Parent: Maybe you could think again and see what your brain can discover.
Child: My brain says maybe it's because a boat came by and made waves.
Parent: A boat could have made the waves. Now your brain is working and coming up with some guesses. Do you have any more ideas?

An Alphabet Soup of Suggesting Hypotheses Activities

a. How come on some days the moon is full and on other days it looks like a crescent? What hypotheses can you suggest to explain it?
b. How come the ocean has so many waves?
c. How come mother's plant on the windowsill is losing its leaves?
d. How come some dogs are friendly and some growl when they see you?
e. How come it's so hard to learn to ride a two-wheeler bike?
f. How come a big ship can float on top of the water, but a little rock will sink to the bottom?
g. How do you suppose the dog knows when its time for you to come home from school and sits by the door and waits?
h. How come dogs are easier to train than cats?
i. How come brothers and sisters fight so much?
j. How come some kids are bullies?
k. How come some kids get a lot of cavities in their teeth?
l. How come some people are afraid of thunder?
m. How come it's easier for some people to learn to play the piano and for some people it's so hard?

n.   How come some people are afraid of mice?

o.   How come some people are afraid of the dark?

p.   How do children choose their friends? What hypotheses can you suggest to explain how that works?

q.   How come some trees lose all their leaves in the fall and other trees keep their leaves on all winter?

r.   How do you explain the reasons we choose certain kinds of clothes? What hypotheses can you suggest to explain our choices?

s.   How come certain books are so popular?

t.   How come some children enjoy computer games so much?

u.   How come some kids hate broccoli?

v.   How did it happen that cell phones became so important in our lives? How can you explain it?

w.   How come some people don't bother to recycle their papers and containers?

x.   How come some people refused to wear their masks to keep them from getting COVID-19? How do you explain it?

y.   Where does the water go when it evaporates? What ideas do you have that would explain it?

z.   How come science is so important to our lives? What are your ideas about that?

NOTES TO PARENTS ABOUT
IMAGINING ACTIVITIES

The operation of imagining has few constraints. Children are asked to let their minds wander to create beautiful, fanciful creations that the mind invents. Imagining may have no basis in reality; it exercises that part of the mind that is frequently untapped in academic work.

But imagination is so important. Wilbur and Orville Wright built the first airplane. But before they could build it, they had to imagine what it would be like to create a machine that could stay up in the air and not fall down.

Hans Christian Anderson wrote some wonderful stories for children. But first, he had to imagine what kinds of stories children would like before he wrote The Ugly Duckling and The Red Shoes.

Alan Turing imagined that he could build a machine to decode secret messages, and he built the first computer.

In asking children to do some imagining activities they may respond by talking about what they invent, or they may draw some pictures of their ideas.

An Alphabet Soup of Imagining Activities

a.   What would it be like to walk on the moon?

b.   What would it be like to have your very own robot?

c.   Imagine that you were a baby robin just hatched out of an egg.

d.   Draw a picture of the strangest tree that you can think of.

e.   What would it be like to take a trip in a hot air balloon?

f.   What would it be like if you were lost in the woods?

g.   What if today were a day that birds could talk? What would they say?

h.   What if today were a day when gravity didn't work? What would that be like?

i.   Where would you go if you could take a trip to anywhere in the world?

j.   What would it be like if you could make yourself invisible?

k.   What would it be like if you could be Cinderella for a day?

l.   What if you had a baby chimp for a pet?

m.   Can you think of something to invent? What would it look like? What would it be able to do?

n.   What if there were no rules we had to obey? What would our lives be like?

o.   Can you think of a different piece of equipment for the playground that would be fun to use?

p.   Can you dream up a story about a pig that could talk?

q.   Can you invent a magic wand that turned bullies into nice people? How would that work?

r.   Can you imagine what your life would be like if you lived in an igloo in the North Pole?

s.   Can you invent a new kind of pizza? What would it look like? What would you put on it?

t.   Can you invent a new style of house that is different from any
        other house you have ever seen? Draw a picture of it.
u.   Draw a picture of a hurricane.
v.   Draw a picture of a sea monster that lives at the bottom of the
        ocean.
w.   Draw a picture of anger.
x.   What if you were the fastest runner in the world? What would
        your life be like?
y.   Make up your own song with music and words.
z.   Make up your own poem about the fog.

NOTES TO PARENTS ABOUT
DECISION-MAKING ACTIVITIES

Choosing is one of the more pervasive acts of living. Almost every
action requires choices to be made. The decisions may be explicit or
implicit; they may involve trivialities or matters of life and death. Even
choosing not to choose is a choice.

Knowing how to choose wisely (and sometimes courageously) is not
a trait we are born with. It has to be learned through experience and
reflection on that experience. Yet, even as adults, we sometimes still
make unwise choices. And some adults tend to repeat those inappropri-
ate choices over and over again. Somehow, they have missed opportunities to learn to choose wisely.

Learning to choose wisely comes with the repeated opportunity to do
just that, followed by a thoughtful and non-defensive examination of
how and why the choice was made. In other words, practice and reflection on action.

When children have learned the habits of making more intelligent
choices, they are being given life skills that will enable them to live
more mature, thoughtful, productive, and compassionate lives.

The purpose of the activities in this section is to help children look at
the choices they make and to examine possible consequences of those
decisions, to themselves and to others. Under such self-scrutiny, children learn a little more about themselves, what kind of persons they are,
and what they hold important. This kind of intelligent examination of
choice enables them to learn more about what they believe to be right
and wrong; what they care for and what is of less value; what they prize
and what they disdain.

It would not be an exaggeration to claim that such intelligent habits of mind promote responsibility, and mature adulthood.

In offering your child an opportunity to choose, it is important to follow that up with a parent-child discussion that asks for what lies behind the choice, why it is important, and what some consequences might be. This is done in the absence of judgment, either negative or affirming the child's decision. The activities are presented in the form of dilemmas.

An example of a parent-child discussion (see the first activity below):

Parent: Tell me what you have decided about what Jane should do.
Child: I think she should just tell Patsy to get off the swing. It's somebody else's turn.
Parent: She should just tell Patsy to get off.
Child: Yeh. Just tell her. In a nice way.
Parent: You think that telling her in a nice way would help.
Child: Yeh. Because if you yell at her, she'd just get mad and stay on the swing longer.
Parent: Yelling is not a good way to tell her.
Child: Yelling is rude.
Parent: You think yelling is rude. You'd not like it if someone yelled at you.
Child: Yeh. Just ask her nicely.
Parent: You are a person who would rather be nice than rude?
Child: Yeh.

An Alphabet Soup of Decision-Making Activities

a. Jane has been on the swing a long time and Patsy wants a turn. What should Patsy do?

b. Harold found a kitten in his garden. It may be lost. Harold has always wanted a kitten. What should he do?

c. Dylan saw his little brother crossing the street when he is not supposed to do that. What should Dylan do?

d. Samantha's mother is calling her home for dinner. But she wants to finish her game with her friends. What should she do?

e. My sister hurt my feelings. What should I do?

f. Harlan is a new boy on the block. He doesn't have any friends. What should he do?

g. I like to have my stuffed bear with me when I go to bed. My sister says I'm a sissy. What should I do?

h. I saw Jun kicking the neighbor's dog. What should I do?

i.   Should you stick up for another boy when you see him being bullied?

j.   My friend says I don't have to wear a mask when I go to the playground. But my mother says I must. What should I tell my friend?

k.   My grandma baked some cookies. I think she must have forgotten to put any sugar in them. I don't want to hurt her feelings. What should I tell her?

l.   Audrey wants to be my friend. But I don't like her. She's mean. What should I do?

m.   Is it okay to tell a little lie?

n.   Sometimes, when someone hurts my feelings, I cry. My sister says I'm a crybaby. What should I tell her?

o.   My friends are going to take a big walk to the park. My mother says I can't go because it's too far. What should I do?

p.   All my friends have tablets. I want one too, but my mother says it costs too much money. What should I tell her?

q.   My father says I can only play on my tablet for half an hour. I want more time. What should I do?

r.   I like to stay up later, but my mother says I have to go to bed at 8:30. What should I tell her?

s.   Colin told me a secret and he said not to tell anyone. But I think it's important to tell my mother. What should I do?

t.   My mother says my room is a mess and I should get in there and clean it up. But this is the time for my favorite TV show. What should I do?

u.   My friends want me to go on the high swings in the playground. But I'm afraid. I don't want them to call me a fraidy cat. What should I do?

v.   I saw Marla taking the candy from Robbie's backpack. Should I tell on her? What should I do?

w.   Pham is a new boy in our class. He can't speak English yet and no one wants to play with him. What should I do?

x.   Our class collected $75 to donate to people who need help. To whom should we give the money?

y.   We were all asked to wear masks to keep us safe during the COVID-19 pandemic. But Brian's mother said he didn't need to wear one. What should I tell Brian?

z.   Some of the boys were throwing stones at the baby ducklings. They are bigger than me. What should I do?

NOTES TO PARENTS ABOUT
PROBLEM-SOLVING ACTIVITIES

Although designing investigation and problem-solving tasks incorporate several of the thinking operations, they are not delineated in the activities that are offered here. The problems are presented in short scenarios to give a fuller perspective of the situations. Once again, no "right answers" are expected or required. The important issue is for the child to consider the situation and to come up with potentially useful solutions—solutions that make sense to him or her. In other words, the child's best thinking.

Once the child has presented his or her response, further thinking is encouraged by the parent's interactive dialogue about not only the solution itself but also about the nature of the thinking process that was underlying the response. It is important, in this interactive dialogue, that no value judgments are made and that parents do not lead the child to the "right answer." An example of how this might work is offered here. The interactive dialogue is preceded by an example of one of the problem-solving scenarios.

Scenario: The local library has been closed to prevent the spread of COVID-19. It has been closed for two months. Robin, who liked to go to the library every week to get new books, is now left without anything new to read. What ideas do you have to help Robin solve his problem?

Philippa: I think we should do a trade.
Parent: You are suggesting that Robin could contact some of his friends to see if they might trade some of their books with him.
Philippa: Yeh. They could trade their books with him and he could trade his books with them.
Parent: I wonder how that could work? What ideas do you have about that?
Philippa: Well, I know he should not go to their house. But maybe they could leave the books at his door and he could leave his books at their door.
Parent: He could leave his books at their door and they could leave their books at his door.
Philippa: Yeh. Kinda like a trade.
Parent: They would be trading books with each other.

Philippa: Yea. They could get some new books to read that way.

Parent: I wonder if you can see some difficulties with that. I mean, do you see any problems arising from that trading?

Philippa: Well, I don't know. Maybe if they left the book on the doorstep, someone might come and take them.

Parent: If you left the books unguarded at the door, someone might take them?

Philippa: Yea. Some bad person who steals.

Parent: So I wonder how you might prevent that from happening?

A Group of Problem-Solving Activities

a. Lee just got a new puppy. He's very happy. But he is responsible for taking care of it. He wants to train it so that it doesn't pee on the floor. But puppies are very frisky and hard to teach new things. How would you solve that problem?

b. Lots of kids had to stay indoors during the time we were all trying to stay safe and not get sick. Schools were closed; the libraries, the playgrounds, and lots of the shops were closed too. What would be a good way for kids to spend their time when they were locked down at home? How would you solve that problem?

c. A new girl came to our class. She had just come to this country and couldn't speak English very well. What could kids do to help her become part of the group?

d. Cats are very hard to train. How would you train a cat so that she would not scratch up the furniture? How would you solve that problem?

e. Some kids on your block say bad things about people who are Black. You know this is wrong. What would you do about it? How would you solve that problem?

f. Marsha makes fun of Lucy because Lucy doesn't have nice clothes. You know this is wrong and it hurts Lucy's feelings. What would you do to change Marsha's behavior? How would you solve that problem?

g. You have a big bucket of water sitting in the sink and you want to pour some off so that the bucket is not too heavy to hold. But it's too heavy to lift—so what can you do to remove some of the water from the bucket? What ideas do you have about how to solve that problem?

h.   Your teacher gave you a piece of paper and told you to draw a picture of something you ate for dinner. You didn't bring your pencils or your crayons today. But you want to do your work. How would you solve that problem?

i.   You want to figure out how much a giraffe weighs. How would you go about doing that?

j.   There is a lot of fighting in our group. How can we learn to get along better? How would you solve that problem?

k.   Allan wants to buy a new app for his tablet. But his mother says that he has to find a way to earn some money to buy it for himself. What ideas do you have that would help Allan earn some money? How would you solve that problem?

l.   You need to measure the length of the room. But you don't have a ruler. How would you solve that problem?

m.   Your grandma wants to buy you a new pair of shoes. But you don't know your size. How can you let her know what size shoes she should buy for you? How would you solve that problem?

n.   The geese laid some eggs on the roof and pretty soon, baby goslings hatched out of the eggs. But the crows were watching. Crows thought that baby goslings would make a wonderful lunch. How would you protect the baby goslings from being eaten by the crows? How would you solve that problem?

o.   You don't have a thermometer, but you want to go outside. How can you figure out what kind of clothes you need to wear today? How would you solve that problem?

p.   Robbie measured the length of the room and he found it was twelve meters long. Sally measured it too, and she found it was ten and a half meters long. Who is right? How would you solve the problem of figuring out the length of the room?

q.   How can you figure out how much air is in a balloon? How would you solve that problem?

r.   Take a piece of string, a small stone, and a stick and make a pendulum. Try to figure out how you can make your pendulum keep swinging from side to side. Then, explain how a pendulum works.

CONCLUSION

A large collection of mind-opening activities rooted in seven of the thinking operations have been included in this chapter for pre- and emerging readers. They are not the last word in possible activities that ask students for their ideas, for their conjectures, for their observations, and for their hypotheses. Many more can be generated and if parents wished to do so, they might consider creating some of their own. But the ones included in this chapter should keep children intellectually engaged and give them many opportunities to think outside of the box.

It is reasonable to expect that once even young children learn the habits of intelligent thinking, they will become more thoughtful, more cautious about making wild assumptions, and more capable of differentiating truth from untruth. Intelligent thinking, like any other learned skill, cannot be mastered in a day or a week; these skills take time to grow and become more the way we think and behave. That is why more practice pays off in the long run.

It is not required, but may be a valuable asset if parents want to keep a brief written record of how their child is responding to these activities. Such a record does not have to be extensive, but recording day to day responses, both behavioral and cognitive, will give hard evidence of how a child is progressing along a continuum that reveals the development of their higher-order mental skills.

Chapter 6

Thinking Activities for Middle Grade Students

There are several preconditions that parents need to be aware of in working with middle graders on tasks that call for higher-order thinking.

For children who have had more classroom time and are more advanced in their reading skills (e.g., Grades 4–7), the tasks may be given to them on cards, notebook paper, or orally. The printed word will allow them to study the task carefully and refer to it as needed.

Second, at this developmental stage, children will be able to respond in writing, although it is also possible for them to respond orally, in a dialog with the parent.

Third, it is essential that the parent stand aside and allow the child to do his or her own thinking. Prompts and leading questions should be avoided. The aim is for children to become more able to think for themselves, and to figure things out on their own.

Fourth, children should be encouraged to consider as many responses as they can; learning to step beyond the "single right answer" response may take a bit of time and encouragement.

Fifth, because the range of skills and know-how increases as children move from Grade 4 up to Grade 7, there will be a comparable range of activities—some considerably more accessible and others more complex and demanding. A parent who knows his or her child well will be able to pick from the large numbers of tasks those that seem not only more appropriate but that are individually challenging as well.

Parents should note that there is no "order" in these mental operations; that is, it is not necessary to follow them in the sequence in which they appear, although it can be immediately seen that the operations of observing, comparing, classifying, and hypothesizing are less challenging than those more sophisticated operations of interpreting, judging, and designing projects and investigations.

As well, there is no order to the activities listed under each of the operations. They are not hierarchical. The tasks can be chosen at the parent's discretion.

And on one more note: the work that the children do on these tasks do not only serve to improve their thinking and reasoning skills; they also allow children to become more informed about the subjects being examined. So, for example, when children are asked to make comparisons of a whale and a submarine, the act of comparing insists that they examine the multifaceted features of both, thus informing them more about whales and submarines.

Since "thinking" at the higher-order mental levels is a learned skill, it follows that the more children can exercise their mental faculties in doing these tasks, the more they become thoughtful and reflective, more cautious in offering opinions, less easily led by "hype," and more judicious in their behaviors. These gains don't come in a day or a week but after long-term exposure and practice in higher-order thinking.

NOTES TO PARENTS ABOUT
COMPARING ACTIVITIES

Several activities require a bit of advance preparation—that is, gathering of materials for the child to use in making comparisons. Activities that require advance preparation are marked with an asterisk (*).

Writing the task down on a 3 × 5 index card will allow the child to read it and re-read if necessary, for further clarification. Children may write their responses in a notebook or on a tablet or laptop. Either way allows for keeping a record of their responses over time.

Begin by explaining what comparing involves—that is, finding the ways in which things are alike and the ways in which they are different. Comparing tasks require thoughtful observation of those similarities and differences which are then recorded. When the task is completed, it is always useful to follow it up with a parent-child discussion about the work, including asking questions that call for further thinking about the issues.

A sample dialog follows in which a parent encourages her daughter to consider additional comparative points:

Parent: I see you have looked at the pictures of a sled and a wagon and saw some similarities. Can you tell me about what some of them are?
Doreen: They are both used to carry things.
Parent: Can you say a little more about that?
Doreen: Well, you can carry your dog on a sled if he doesn't want to walk on the snow. And you can carry your toys in a wagon.
Parent: They can both be used to transport things. Can you tell me about some more similarities?
Doreen: Let me think. Oh, I know. They are both close to the ground.
Parent: Both travel close to the ground level.
Doreen: Yeh. And you can hop on a sled and hop in a wagon easily.
Parent: It's easy to get into them.
Doreen: Yeh. I can't think of anything else.
Parent: Okay. What about differences?
Doreen: That's easy. One has wheels and one has runners.
Parent: The sled travels on runners and the wagon on wheels.
Doreen: Yeh. And one is made of wood and the other is made of metal, I think.
Parent: The ones you are looking at: one is made of wood and one of metal?
Doreen: Yeh. You can put two people in the wagon and you can also put two people on the sled. So that's the same, I think.
Parent: You're coming back to notice some more similarities.
Doreen: Yeh. And I can think of some more.
Parent: I'd like to hear them.

An Alphabet Soup of Things to Compare

What are some similarities? What are some differences?

a. Ice hockey and football
b. Sleds and wagons
c. Eels and turtles
d. Whales and submarines
e. Windmills and kites
f. Cell phones and laptops
g. TV and radio
h. Spiders and bees

 i. First grade and fifth grade
 j. Encyclopedia Brown and Sherlock Holmes
 k. Living on a farm and living in a city
 l. Hot dogs and pizza
 m. A painting by Warhol and a painting by Klee* (see, e.g., https ://www.moma.org/learn/moma_learning/andy-warhol-campbells -soup-cans-1962/ and https://en.wikipedia.org/wiki/Fish_Magic _(Klee)
    N. B. The images may be printed out for the child to study.
 n. Feathers and fur
 o. E-mail and regular mail
 p. A police officer and a firefighter
 q. An airport and a railroad station
 r. A doctor and a teacher
 s. Facebook and Twitter
 t. A river and an ocean
 u. Abraham Lincoln and Martin Luther King
 v. The American Revolution and the Civil War
 w. Two advertisements
 x. Columbus and Neil Armstrong (first man on the moon)
 y. Navajos and East Indians
 z. COVID-19 and the Spanish flu

NOTES TO PARENTS ABOUT OBSERVING ACTIVITIES

An important consideration in asking children to make observations is for them to attend to the accuracy of what they see, hear, touch, and smell. That means avoiding making assumptions and judgments and staying faithful to what has been observed. Getting accurate information from observations allows us to become more discerning, more tuned into reality. As we gain skill in the process of making accurate observations, we become more informed about the world in which we live.

Before presenting your child with an observing activity, it is helpful to remind him or her of the nature of what is required in the task—that is, to make accurate observations of what is seen (heard, smelled) avoiding assumptions and opinions. Observations can be recorded on a sheet of paper, in a notebook, or on a laptop or tablet. Activities that require a bit of advance preparation of materials are marked with an asterisk (*).

Children who choose to gather data from a laptop, a tablet, or any other data source should be free to do so. They should also be cautioned about the accuracy of the data gathered from the Internet since a lot of what is there cannot be trusted to be true.

Several activities in the list below provide URLs to an image or a short video of what is to be observed. Parents should perhaps check the URL first before the child embarks on the task, so that the image is clear and any ads that accompany the image can be deleted. Parents should also feel free to substitute another image or video; for example, in the case of the Guernica (Picasso's painting of his impressions of the Spanish Civil War), another painting that is less gruesome is easy to find and serves a comparable purpose of making observations.

When the child has completed the task, it is a good idea to follow that up with a discussion of what has been seen or heard. These post-hoc discussions are important for several reasons. At first, they show that the parent is interested in what the child has done. Second, it provides the parent with some insight into the child's thinking about what has been seen or heard. Third, it allows the parent a chance to ask the kinds of questions that would promote more intelligent thought about the observation.

In these post-hoc discussions, parents should avoid, in so far as possible, any kind of judgment—since such responses are more than likely to torque a child's responses in the direction of parental approval, rather than giving him or her a chance to think for him/herself. That includes, "that's interesting."

A sample of a parent-child interactive discussion shows how a parent enables the child's thinking about the observations that have been made.

Parent: You made some observations about what you saw in the supermarket. And you wrote down some of your observations. Can you tell me about them?
Ruben: There were a lot of people buying stuff. The carts were full of stuff.
Parent: You observed people buying a lot of groceries?
Ruben: Not only groceries. But other stuff too.
Parent: Can you tell me about the other stuff?
Ruben: Well, there was some dog food and I saw someone buying a big package of toilet paper.

Parent: So people buy other things than groceries at the market. Like dog food and paper goods.
Ruben: Yeh.
Parent: What other observations did you make at the market?
Ruben: Some little kids got to ride in the carts. They get wheeled around.
Parent: Some parents keep their kids in the cart. I wonder how this helps?
Ruben: I think so they don't get lost.
Parent: A little kid could get lost in the market.
Ruben: Yeh.
Parent: Any other observations?
Ruben: Well there are a lot of aisles. It's a very big place.
Parent: A supermarket has a lot of space with a lot of aisles full of stuff.
Ruben: Yeh.
Parent: I wonder if you observed any smells or sounds.

An Alphabet Soup of Observing Activities

Ask the child to:

a. Close your eyes for a minute and make some observations of the sounds heard.
b. Look out the window of the room and make some observations of what is seen outside.
c. Remember what you saw on a trip to the supermarket. What was observed?
d. Think about what you saw when your mother or father was preparing dinner. What was observed?
e. Think about what you have to do to train a dog to sit up. What observations can you make about that?
f. Make some observations of the ways in which certain foods are prepared, like making bread or pizza.
g. Listen for the sounds of a particular musical instrument and make some observations of those sounds.
h. Make some observations of a character in a story you like for example, Harry Potter. What can you say about that character that is an accurate description?
i. Make some observations of a character in a story that was a villain, for example, Captain Hook in *Peter Pan*. What can you say about that character that is an accurate description?

j. Make some observations of the way you compute double-digit multiplication and long division examples and describe the process you use to find the answer.

k. Make some observations of the behavior of an animal (or animals) in a zoo. What can you say about their behavior?

l. Study the famous painting of Guernica, by Picasso. What observations can you make about what you see here? (https://wallpapercave. com/guernica-wallpaper)

m. Study the image of the crab. What observations can you make about this animal? (https://www.gettyimages.ca/detail/photo/crab-royalty-free-image/182150336?adppopup=true)

n. Study the image of an octopus. What observations can you make about this animal? (https://www.gettyimages.ca/photos/octopus ?mediatype=photography&phrase=octopus&sort=mostpopular)

o. Study the image of Darth Vader. What observations can you make about it? (https://www.shutterstock.com/image-photo/san-bened etto-del-tronto-italy-may-280768850)

p. You will need a pan, with water, and a bunch of objects that you can drop in the water and see which sink and which float. Then, make some observations of which objects sink and which float. Make some observations of how you can turn a sinker into a floater.*

q. You will need to gather some small rocks and stones for this activity. Lay them out and make some observations about what you see.*

r. Make some observations of this bird building a nest. What did you observe? (https://www.youtube.com/watch?v=g1zCj3Tltxw)

s. Make some observations of the circulatory system in the human body. (https://www.thinglink.com/scene/747675543704436738)

t. Collect these materials: rubber bands, string, scissors, fine wire, a few cans, a few cardboard containers, and a stapler. Use the materials to make some stringed instruments. What kinds of sounds can be made on each? Make some observations of the sounds and how they are produced. *

u. Observe the images of the human skeleton. What observations can you make? (https://www.istockphoto.com/ca/photo/male-human-sk eleton-four-views-front-back-side-and-perspective-gm135853422 -18613886)

v. Collect these materials: small pieces of tissue paper, a comb, a few pieces of fabric (wool, nylon, cotton, silk), and balloons. Use these materials to find out about static electricity. Then write your observations about how this works. *

w. Study the map of Canada. What observations can you make about this large country from looking at the map? (https://www.amazon.c a/Fun-Time-Canada-Kids-Rugs/dp/B005HOL7FQ)

x. Have a look at the video of a Navajo dancer. What observations can you make about this tribal ceremony? (https://www.youtube.com/w atch?v=hDUKemNCW58)

y. Make some observations about the different ways in which tablets are used.

z. Make some observations about the different ways in which we use water.

NOTES TO PARENTS ABOUT CLASSIFYING ACTIVITIES

Classifying activities are perhaps more easily done than many of the others, since children are called on to classify many times in their lives. For example, they know the drawers in which socks, underwear, shirts, and pants belong. They know on which shelves to place their toys when asked to clean up their room. They know, in school, that reading, math, science, and recess come at certain hours of the day. Classifying helps us to bring some order into our often chaotic lives.

As in other thinking activities, there are no right answers to classifying. The essential aim of classifying is ensuring there is a purpose to how the groups are formed. So just grouping things helter-skelter won't be as effective a strategy as grouping with an overall purpose.

Some activities begin by asking the child to make a list of certain things. In making their lists, children should feel free to gather data from Internet sources. There are benefits to that kind of inquiry, not the least is learning to use resources to find needed information.

In responding to a child's classification system, it is helpful to follow up with a discussion that brings to light the nature of his or her thinking. Such discussions also enable the parent to raise questions that call for deeper analysis of what has been done.

For example:

Parent: You made a list of the different ways people communicate with each other and then you classified them. Your list included cell phones, landline phones, letters, e-mail, Skype and Zoom, TV, and some others.

Kim: Yes. I had more on my list too. But when I started to group them, I could see that some needed electronics and some didn't. So that was one kind of group.

Parent: Some types of communication required the use of electronic devices. Others didn't. That was one kind of grouping. How does it help you to know that?

Kim: Well, for example, if you didn't have access to batteries or an outlet to boot up your electronic device, you'd be out of luck.

Parent: So one way of classifying shows what you would need in order to use some of these communication devices.

Kim: Well, of course, if you are using the regular mail, you'd need access to a post office. And that might be a problem

Parent: Even using regular mail has some limitations.

Kim: Yeh. There's also another way to classify, and that is according to how fast a message can get through. A cell phone or e-mail sends your message faster. And that is why they call the postal service "snail mail."

Parent: Another way of classifying is by considering how long it would take for a message to get through. Speed.

Kim: Yeh. I can think of another way, and that is cost. It costs more to own a cell phone or a laptop to send messages. And the post office only needs a stamp—just a few cents.

Parent: Cost is another factor, another way of classifying forms of communication. You haven't listed putting a message in a bottle and throwing it into the sea.

Kim: That's funny, Mom.

An Alphabet Soup of Classifying Activities

Ask the child to put the following into related groups:

a. Elephant, hippo, giraffe, lion, tiger, chimpanzee, snake, turtle, crocodile, raccoon, squirrel, duck, swan, goose, zebra, panda, leopard, deer, polar bear, black bear, cheetah, rhino, peacock, koala, camel, wolf, rabbit, pig, mouse, owl, reindeer, horse

b. Corn, lima beans, apple pie, strawberries, potatoes, chocolate cake, peanuts, bread, lamb chops, honey, ice cream, peas, radish, squash, eggs, fish, orange, ham, oysters, cheese, walnuts, chicken, waffle, milk, carrots, cantaloupe, rice, string beans, bacon, hot dog, pizza, hamburger, steak, cauliflower, shrimp

c. Kilometer, foot, yard, ruler, pint, acre, liter, inch, ounce, meter, Fahrenheit, gram, Celsius, yardstick, thermometer, pound, kilogram, hectare, mile, scale, gallon, quart, measuring cup

d. a, b, c, d, e, f, g, h, i, j, k, l, m, n, o, p, q, r, s, t, u, v, w, x, y, z

e. Soupspoon, fork, salad fork, butter knife, bread knife, ladle, tongs, oven mitt, toaster, frying pan, soup kettle, tea kettle, toaster oven, microwave oven, oven thermometer, blender, mixer, can opener, teapot, mug, cup, saucer

f. Piano, harp, violin, drum, flute, clarinet, trombone, viola, oboe, trumpet, guitar, ukelele, banjo, cello, saxaphone, accordian, harmonica, recorder, bassoon, tuba, bagpipes

First make a list of the following. Then classify the items.

g. Human residences

h. Different holidays across the world

i. All the vehicles you can think of

j. All the apps you can think of

k. The many different kinds of diseases that people can get

l. All the ways of collecting information you can think of

m. All the books you have read in the last few months

n. All the ways we use to transport things (people, goods, materials)

o. All the insects you can think of

p. All the wars the United States has been engaged in in the last 200 years

q. The different ways in which people communicate with each other

r. All the creatures that live in the sea

s. All the different kinds of tools you can think of

t. All the different kinds of activities you do in school during the whole term

u. All the organs in the human body you can think of

v. The states in the United States

w. The different kinds of garbage that is thrown away in your house every day

x. The different kinds of things you do for fun

y. A dozen ads you've seen on TV

z. The different things kids do for recreation

NOTES FOR PARENTS ABOUT
HYPOTHESIZING ACTIVITIES

By the intermediate grades, most children will have an appreciation of what it means to suggest hypotheses. For those for whom this is a new concept, a starting point would be to explain what hypotheses are: certain kinds of guesses that might lead to an explanation of things we don't understand.

For example: In certain countries, the incidence of deaths due to COVID-19 was considerably greater than in other countries. Brazil, the United States, and Russia had a much higher number of cases. Canada, Sweden, and Australia had much fewer cases. What hypotheses can you suggest that explain such differences?

Scientists who study that data offer hypotheses that help them not only to explain the difference but also to point to ways in which they can use that information to prevent further illness. That is why the ability to come up with reasonable hypotheses can help us not only in matters of scientific endeavors but also in dealing with some problems in our everyday lives.

What's important in generating hypotheses is that they be credible— that is, that they attend, in a meaningful way, to potential solutions to a problem. Children should be encouraged to come up with several hypotheses and then identify the one or several that are the most reasonable in leading toward a solution to the problem.

Once the child has done the task, it is always valuable for the parent to discuss the ways in which the child has dealt with the activity. This has several benefits: it acknowledges and affirms the importance of what the child has done; it gives the parent insight into the nature of the child's thinking; and not the least important, it gives the parent a chance to extend the child's thinking, to dig more deeply, to discern the logic and the validity of his or her responses.

As in all these discussions, parents should avoid making judgments, offering praise, agreeing, correcting—all "traps" that do more to constrain children's thinking than advance it.

It will become immediately apparent that beginning with the mental operation of hypothesizing, the activities offered in an a to z sequence have become more challenging, many of them dealing with more current and perhaps more serious situations. Among them are also a few that are less so—and once again, parents are the best informed with respect to choosing tasks for their children.

Example of parent-child dialog:

Parent: You were working on the problem of the Salem Witch Trials and I'd like to hear what hypotheses you came up with to explain how come people at that time believed in witches.

Aubrey: We studied that in school, and I remember a little bit about it. I think it was because they didn't have the information they needed to explain things they couldn't understand.

Parent: The time that this took place, in the 1600s, people's knowledge was more limited?

Aubrey: Yes. They didn't have good science. They didn't have good medicine. So when something weird happened, like a drought or a tornado, they thought it was caused by witchcraft.

Parent: When you don't have good science to help you understand phenomena, you look to the paranormal?

Aubrey: Yeh. That's one thing that happened.

Parent: You have some other hypotheses to explain it?

Aubrey: Yeh. People in those times thought that the devil was responsible for bad things that happened.

Parent: They believed in the devil?

Aubrey: Yeh. If bad things happened, it was the devil that did it.

Parent: I wonder where that idea came from? The idea that the devil was behind all the bad things?

Aubrey: They had no other information. How could you explain why bad things happened if you didn't have science to help you understand it?

Parent: So once again, you are pointing to the lack of knowledge, and especially to the lack of understanding of science that allowed them to believe in witches.

Aubrey: Yeh. It's ignorance.

Parent: Ignorance leads to misinformation and belief in the devil?

Aubrey: Yeh.

Parent: So perhaps given that hypotheses, one way to address that problem is by teaching people more about science.

Aubrey: The more information you have, the more you know. Science helps us to know more about more things.

Parent: I see you are pretty clear about that. I want to raise one more issue. How come, in your opinion, it was women who were accused of witchcraft, and never men?

An Alphabet Soup of Activities that
Call for Hypothesizing

a. Why do you suppose some children like to spend so much time on their tablets? What hypotheses can you suggest to explain it?

b. Martin Luther King was an American minister and activist who became an admired leader in the civil rights movement. What, in your view, made it possible for King to become such a good leader?

c. Some children hold views that might be called "racist." Where do you suppose they get those ideas? What hypotheses do you have that explains it?

d. During the COVID-19 pandemic, some people chose not to wear masks to protect themselves and others, even though wearing masks was strongly advised by the doctors. What hypotheses can you suggest to explain it?

e. In several countries, the incidence of the COVID-19 disease was greater than in others. Brazil, the United States, and Russia had many more cases than Sweden, Canada, and Australia. What hypotheses can you suggest to explain those differences?

f. Your neighbor's dog has not eaten in two days. He is not active. He will not even chase cats. The vet cannot be reached. What do you think may be the problem? What hypotheses can you suggest?

g. You are working on a math problem involving division of fractions. The answer you get is incorrect. What do you suppose the problem might be? What hypotheses can you suggest?

h. Why do you think a ball bounces? What hypotheses can you suggest to explain it?

i. Why do countries make war? What hypotheses can you suggest to explain it?

j. Why do you suppose it is harder to climb uphill than walking on a straight path? What hypotheses can you suggest?

k. Carl is a bully. He punches, kicks, and makes fun of other kids. How come? What hypotheses can you suggest to explain his behavior?

l. Molly wants to get all her information about the news from one source in the Internet. You think that some of what she sees and hears is disinformation and what's worse, she believes all of that. What do you suppose you can do to help her?

m. Arnold thinks he's the smartest kid in the class. He also thinks he's the most handsome. He also believes that everyone likes him. The truth is that he is not the smartest, nor the most handsome; and in fact, few people do like him. What hypotheses can you suggest to explain why he believes these things about himself?

n. Why do you suppose Facebook is so popular? What hypotheses can you suggest to explain it?

o. When Ruby Bridges, aged five, began her first day at school, she needed four Federal Marshalls to walk with her. She was the first Black child to enter an all-white school. Many white people stood by and yelled at her. Some threw things. Why do you suppose all those people were against Ruby's going to that school? What hypotheses can you suggest to explain it?

p. Some children dislike sports. Some love sports. How do you explain people's choices?

q. During the time of Westward Expansion in the United States, Native Americans were removed from their land to make more space for the white settlers. What hypotheses can you suggest for how the U.S. government to allow this to happen?

r. During World War II, the U.S. and Canadian governments gathered up American and Canadian citizens who were of Japanese descent and put them in prison camps. What hypotheses can you suggest to explain why these governments did that?

s. Why do you suppose some people believe in ghosts? What hypotheses can you suggest to explain it?

t. Two football players earned more than $100 million dollars each last year. Two teachers each earned $20,000 last year. How do you explain the huge differences in salaries of teachers and football players? What hypotheses can you suggest?

u. What is it about dogs that make them such good pets? What hypotheses can you suggest to explain it?

v. In the southern states in the United States, it was legal for people there to own slaves. These people believed that it was their right to own Black people to work on their farms, plantations, and in their homes. The slaves did not get any salary for their work. How was it possible for people to believe that it was OK for them to own Black people? What hypotheses can you suggest to explain it?

w. What explains our fascination with space travel? What hypotheses can you suggest?

x. What explains some adult's willingness to believe fake news? What hypotheses can you suggest?

y. Why do you suppose the painting by Van Gogh (who never sold a painting in his life) sold for $20 million dollars? What hypotheses can you suggest?

z. What, in your view, explains why people in Salem, Massachusetts, in 1692, believed in witches and burned some women alive because they thought they were witches? What hypotheses can you suggest?

NOTES TO PARENTS ABOUT IMAGINING ACTIVITIES

From the more sophisticated and more challenging activities in the above section on hypothesizing, the work on imagining activities takes a breather. In these activities, children are free to invent, to create, to imagine—to go outside the box and to dream of what can be, rather than of what is.

Before the work in this operation is dismissed as less productive, it is helpful to remember that many of the more advanced strides that have been made in science, medicine, physics, astronomy, architecture, art, and other areas have their roots in those men and women who dreamed of what could be possible, rather than what was already there.

Alan Turing, the man responsible for the invention of the first computer, imagined that he could build a machine that would be able to decode the very sophisticated German coding apparatus, The Enigma machine.

Amelia Earhart dreamed that she could be the first woman to fly solo across the Atlantic Ocean.

Ruby Bridges believed she could be the first Black child to enroll in an all-white school in Louisiana.

Martin Luther King believed he could be a voice to inspire American Black people to stand up for their civil rights.

Christopher Columbus dreamed he could sail across the Atlantic Ocean to find a short route to India.

Michelangelo dreamed he could paint a religious scene on the ceiling of the Sistine Chapel in Rome.

J. K. Rowling dreamed of a character named Harry Potter who would be a hero to millions of children reading her books.

From the dreams and beliefs in their dreams of people throughout history, great advances have been made to our thinking and to the advancement of our cultures.

That is one reason that imagining activities are so important and one reason that they should not be overlooked in promoting children's higher-order thinking skills.

Once again, giving your child an opportunity to discuss what he or she has envisioned in a parent-child dialog that examines the nature of the thinking that went into the work should not be neglected.

An Alphabet Soup of Imagining Activities

a. Make up two jokes that will make someone laugh.
b. Make up a cartoon that will show how you feel about sports.
c. Draw a picture of what you think the car of the future will look like.
d. What do you think houses will look like 100 years from now? Draw some pictures of them.
e. Imagine you were stationed in an Arctic weather station for a year. What would your life be like? Write a short description of it.
f. What was life like aboard the ship Mayflower as it sailed from England to the New World in 1619? Write a poem about it.
g. What would a day's life be like if you were a crocodile? Write a short story about it.
h. If you could invent a description of the best teacher in the world, what would that teacher be like? Write a short description of that person.
i. If your dog could talk, what would he or she say?
j. What would it be like to spend two months in a space satellite?
k. Suppose you were among the people who traveled across the United States in covered wagons. What would a day in that life be like?
l. What does the world look like through the experiences of a worm? How would you describe it?
m. What would it be like to be a slave working on a plantation in the south before the Civil War? Write a short story about it.
n. How would you create the perfect dessert? Draw a picture of it.
o. Design your idea of the perfect garden. Draw a picture of it.
p. Invent six words that would describe the most horrible tasting food you ever ate.

q. Invent six words that would describe the most beautiful scene you ever saw.
r. Design your idea of the most perfect playground. Draw a picture of it.
s. What would be a most important invention that would benefit the world? Write a story about it.
t. Suppose Columbus had not "discovered" America. What would the world look like now?
u. If you could live wherever you wanted, where would that be? Write a short poem about it.
v. Create a script for a science fiction movie.
w. Invent a song that would become a number one hit.
x. Design a musical instrument that would be easy for beginners to learn to play.
y. Design a stage set for the play *The Emperor's New Clothes*. Draw a picture of it.
z. Design a new app for a tablet that would be fun and educational.

NOTES TO PARENTS ABOUT DECISION-MAKING ACTIVITIES

Choosing is one of the more pervasive acts of life. From the moment we awake in the morning to the time we go to bed, we engage in many acts of choosing. Choices can be mundane: shall I wear my blue dress or my pantsuit? Shall I put my hair up or let it hang loose? Shall I poach some eggs or just make do with toast?

Or they can be profound: Who will get my vote to be the next president? How will I manage to stretch my food budget for the rest of the week? What charities will get the largest donation? How will I manage to educate my daughter while she is out of school during the lockdown of the COVID-19 pandemic? What are the best strategies to teach my children about racism?

Children, even at young ages, engage in decision making, although they may not be aware of doing so. They choose their clothes, their foods, their friends, their recreational activities, their games, their apps, and the nature of their interactions with others. In the higher-order mental operation of decision making, the object is to promote children's greater awareness of the decisions they make—what's behind them, what's important, how the choice was made, and what the consequences of those decisions are. In other words, to bring decision making into their conscious awareness.

Once again, as children engage in choosing, there are no "right choices." This is where the "rubber hits the road." Except in matters of health and safety, parents will need to hold back their temptation to urge or lead a child to the "right" decision. And that is not easy, because we all want our kids to make the "right" choice. But in these exercises, what's more important is to allow the child the right to choose for him or herself and to bring that decision under examination. When children become more consciously aware of their decisions, they become more thoughtful, more reasonable, more in tune with how those decisions impact themselves and others. Having reflected on those choices, children learn a little more about themselves—what kind of persons they are, what they believe in, and what they stand for.

And that is one primary objective of the decision-making activities.

A sample of a parent-child discussion after the child has chosen follows:

Parent: You were thinking about what to do at the park during the time when social distancing was important, and you saw some people who were not doing that.

Ruth: Yeh. I remember when that happened too. When we were in the park and keeping apart from each other.

Parent: You saw some people who were not keeping apart?

Ruth: Yeh. I didn't do anything. I just kept away from them.

Parent: You didn't think it was a good idea for you to say anything to them?

Ruth: Well, they were older. They should know better.

Parent: You were surprised that they didn't know better?

Ruth: Yeh. When people do that, it makes us all less safe.

Parent: People who didn't follow the social distancing rules made us all feel less safe?

Ruth: Yeh. That's why so many people were getting sick from the virus.

Parent: So perhaps something should have been done about the people you saw?

Ruth: I wish a policeman would come and tell them.

Parent: But you didn't do it yourself. Tell them.

Ruth: I was afraid. They were grown up and I'm just a kid.

Parent: Being younger means you can't approach adults who are behaving badly.

Ruth: It's not my job to tell them.

Parent: Whose job is it?

Ruth: I don't know. The police I think.

Parent: And if the police are not available?

Ruth: Maybe some other grown-up person.

Parent: But not you?

Ruth: No. But if I was older, maybe I would.

Parent: I see.

An Alphabet Soup of Decision-Making Activities

a. Cicely wants to join the study group, but the others in the group don't want her. What should she do?

b. Lee saw his best friend taking some candy from another child's backpack. What should Lee do?

c. Donald told Lewis that he could copy all of his homework assignments from what is posted on the Internet. What should Lewis tell Donald?

d. Keith is going to be late for school. He overslept. He knows his teacher is going to be angry. What should he tell his teacher?

e. Stephen broke his friend's skateboard. What should Stephen do?

f. Marie's grandfather went to a lot of trouble to make her a special dish for her lunch. Marie tasted it and didn't like it. What should she do?

g. During the time when the COVID-19 pandemic was a serious threat, and people were being asked to keep two meters apart when they were out, Brent saw two boys in the park that were not following the social distance rule. What should he do?

h. The teacher told Tim that it was important for him to do his math homework every day if he hoped to improve his marks. But Tim hated math. What should he do?

i. Audrey's mother wants her to learn to play the violin. But Audrey hates to practice. What should Audrey do?

j. The teacher wants to know what we can do, as a class, to stop racist behavior. What should we tell her?

k. What kinds of friends are important to you? What are some characteristics of those people?

l. What kinds of things would you do so that your friends will like you? Are those good things to do? Will you be glad to do them?

m. Are marks in school important to you? What would you be prepared to do to get good marks?

n. You wanted a new app for your tablet, but your dad said that you already had more apps than was necessary. What should you do now?

o. What are some of the things you do (or did) when you have to stay home from school? What did you see as some consequences of those activities?

p. How do you see yourself becoming a more thoughtful person? What suggestions can you make about what you might do?

q. Cheryl saw some big boys throwing rocks at a dog. She was afraid to tell them to stop, but she didn't want the dog to be hurt. What should she do?

r. Your teacher has asked for volunteers to read stories to kindergarten children. What stories would you choose? Why would you pick those stories?

s. Brian's mother told him that he needed to babysit his younger brother while she went to the market. What should Brian do to keep the boy from getting into mischief while mother was away?

t. The teacher told her Grade 6 class that they were not following the class rules of good behavior. What should the teacher do?

u. Sally's parents were taking her on a picnic on Saturday, and she asked her friend Shawana to come. But Shawana's parents said she couldn't go. What should Shawana do?

v. William saw some big boys making fun of an old man in ragged clothes. What should William do?

w. The teacher wanted the class to make some contributions to others in need. How should the class go about finding out who was in need? What kinds of contributions should the class make?

x. Most of the other children in Gary's class had their own cell phones. Gary wanted one too. What should he tell his parents in order to persuade them to buy one for him?

y. Kevin saw some grown-up people throwing their trash on the grass in the park. What should Kevin do?

z. How do children learn how to become more polite and less rude? What ideas do you have about that?

NOTES TO PARENTS ABOUT
IDENTIFYING ASSUMPTIONS

Assumptions are those ideas, behaviors, strategies, and situations that we take for granted. Assumptions are not necessarily wrong; what is important is to be able to see the difference between what is assumed and what is patently true or false.

To be able to differentiate between what is assumed to be true and what is observable fact is at the very heart of logical reasoning. When children develop their skills in identifying assumptions, they are less likely to fall prey to the seductive qualities of the advertiser, or the manufacturer, or the politician who asks for your vote. Children will be less likely to accept propaganda as fact, experimental data as proof, or conclusions as "right." They will be less likely to leap to conclusions based on limited data and less impulsive in their actions.

Why is this so important among the operations that call for more intelligent habits of mind?

More than ever before in our history, children and adults are bombarded with "news" in a twenty-four-hour cycle. News comes on the radio, on TV, and on the Internet. Items of "news" come on Facebook and Instagram. Because most of the news comes from what is considered reliable sources, it's easy to believe that what we see and hear is based in truth. "Scam" telephone calls ask for our closely guarded information—how do we know that those calls actually come from real federal agents and not from some tricksters trying to con us out of our credit card numbers?

Remember what P.T. Barnum said: "There's a sucker born every minute."

When we give our children a chance to develop their critical thinking skills, so that they may be able to suspend judgment and look for what assumptions are being made, we are giving them valuable life-preserving skills. And that is far from an overstatement for the times in which we now live.

As in the other sets of activities, it is helpful to engage your child in a post-hoc discussion after he or she has worked through the activity. Once again, the aim is to stimulate further thought rather than to lead to "correct" answers. An example of one such discussion follows:

Parent: You were working on the activity about the person who wanted to vote for the good looking boy.

Lee: Yes, I know that some people choose a person because he looks good rather than how good a person he is.

Parent: So some assumptions are being made?

Lee: Yeh. I think they assume that if a person is good looking, he is a good person.

Parent: I wonder how such an assumption is made? Do you have any ideas about it?

Lee: Well, I think it's because we are attracted to people who are better looking.

Parent: We like the way they look, so we like them better?

Lee: Yes. That's what happens, I think.

Parent: How does such an assumption cause us trouble?

Lee: Well, a good looking person can be a very bad person too. How you look doesn't make you a better person.

Parent: You don't see a connection between good looks and good behavior?

Lee: It doesn't have anything to do with anything. You can be a perfectly good person and be ugly.

Parent: Good people can be ugly. And bad people can be handsome?

Lee: Yeh.

Parent: So what would you advise about making an assumption about good looks?

An Alphabet Soup of Identifying Assumption Activities

a. What assumptions do you make when you favor a candidate who is running for president? What assumptions are being made about his or her competence to do the job?

b. Sometimes we make a decision, like choosing an app for your tablet, and we make some assumptions that turn out to be false. Give some examples of this having happened to you.

c. The U.S. Pesticide Control Appeal Board approved the use of TORDAN 22K. This herbicide (plant killer) is to be used by the highways department to control weeds growing at the side of the highway. The Board has issued a statement saying that TORDAN 22K will have no bad effects on humans. What assumptions are being made in the use of this herbicide?

d. What clothes did you choose to wear this morning? What assumptions did you make when you chose those clothes?

e. A small group of people marched down Bay Street protesting the wearing of masks during the COVID-19 pandemic. They were chanting that it was a denial of their freedom to have to wear masks. What assumptions were they making?

f. Some groups of people have been called "primitive." What assumptions are being made by that term?

g. What assumptions are being made when people are referred to as "civilized"?

h. One toothpaste advertisement announces that if you use that brand, you will have 32 percent fewer cavities. What assumptions are they asking you to make?

i. We are experiencing more extreme weather and it's because of global warming. What assumptions are being made by that statement?

j. You can tell if a person is a good citizen if that person has an American flag pin on his jacket. What assumptions are being made?

k. Don said, "I don't need to wear a face mask. The news about the COVID-19 virus is a hoax." What assumptions are being made?

l. What makes cell phones so important in our lives? What assumptions are being made here?

m. What kinds of jobs deserve the highest salaries? What assumptions are being made?

n. How should your school deal with bullies? What assumptions are being made?

o. How should your school deal with racist behavior? What assumptions are being made?

p. Malcolm is so good looking. I'm going to vote for him. What assumptions are being made?

q. In the United States, women were not considered eligible to vote until 1920. The argument was made that women were not capable of making intelligent choices. What assumptions were being made?

r. The laws restricting immigration are based on the belief that immigrants will take jobs away from citizens. What assumptions are being made?

s. "The reason for the American Revolution was taxes." What assumptions are being made?

t. "Men should earn more money than women for the same jobs. They are stronger and work harder." What assumptions are being made here?

u. Tanya's boyfriend asked her to post a selfie on Facebook. Tanya thought that if she did that, he would like her better. What assumptions was she making?

v. The Parks Board closed Stanley Park to all car traffic during the COVID-19 pandemic. What assumptions were being made by that closure?

w. I tried to contact my friend by e-mail but didn't get any answer. What explains that? What assumptions are being made?

x. Mrs. Cooper saw a Black man walking past her house. She phoned the police. What assumptions was she making?

y. What are some good ways to protect ourselves from becoming ill with COVID-19? What assumptions are you making?

z. Where do you think germs come from? What assumptions are you making?

NOTES TO PARENTS ABOUT
INTERPRETING ACTIVITIES

The ability to interpret—that is, to explain the meanings that an experience or a set of data has for us, is one of the more difficult of the higher-order mental operations. Too often, we look at a set of data, a slogan, an illustration, a cartoon, and draw an immediate, but unwarranted conclusion. One reason may be because we are not sufficiently trained to exercise that mental function of making reliable interpretations. Another is that it is much easier to leap to judgment and much more difficult to search within the data to find its essential meaning.

Of course, lacking such interpreting abilities can get us into a lot of trouble.

We look at the scene of spilled milk, the cat licking its paws, and jump to the conclusion: "The cat did it." But reading the data more carefully may lead to another, more reliable interpretation. Going beyond the data is often a cause for deep regret when we act based on faulty interpretations. We may blame perfectly innocent people for a crime; we may conclude that a student who has not finished her work is lazy; we may listen to a speaker and draw the wrong conclusion from her message.

Being able to make appropriate and reliable interpretations gives us an important mental device that enables us to understand more—not only from the surface but from within, which benefits us in many ways. Children who continually misinterpret and miss the meaning are severely handicapped in their ability to understand and may be driven to act unwisely.

Sometimes, when we look at data—a graph, a chart, an illustration, a cartoon, a slogan—we are clear about the meanings. Sometimes, meanings are not clear and when we interpret, we resort to qualifiers, such as probably true or probably false. Sometimes the data are such that we are unable to draw even a tentative interpretation. The bottom line is that the body of data or experience supports the interpretation and that generalizations are not made on the basis of insufficient information.

An important follow-up activity to the student's responses on the tasks below is the parent-child discussion, in which parents can, through the use of facilitative responses and higher-order questions, enable the child to discern more about the experience and bring his or her interpretations more in line with what the data suggest. An example of such a discussion:

Parent: You were working on the interpretation of the protests and signs saying "I can't breathe." What did you make of that?

Ellie: I saw a lot of photos of those protests and I think it's because so many people are sick and tired of how the police are treating Black people.

Parent: You think it's a protest against police violence against Blacks.

Ellie: It's been going on for a long time. I mean, look at the way the police are dressed. They look like they are going to war.

Parent: Even their clothing suggests that they are on the attack?

Ellie: Yeh. Just looking at them makes you afraid.

Parent: Let's get back to your explanation of the protest signs.

Ellie: Okay. I know the signs are saying what the man who was killed was telling the policeman who had his foot on his neck.

Parent: The protest signs are saying what Mr. Floyd said when the police had him pinned down.

Ellie: Yeh. The thing is, my interpretation is that they don't treat Black people the way they treat white people. There's racism against Black people.

Parent: So one interpretation of the protests is against racism by the police?

Ellie: Yeh. But the thing is, I don't know if that is going to help.

Parent: Your interpretation is that protests of this kind don't help to remedy a bad situation. Protests don't stop racism?

Ellie: I don't know. But I'm glad that they are protesting. I'm glad that a lot of people are taking a stand against racism.

An Alphabet Soup Plus One of Interpreting Activities

a. This is an old Cherokee piece of advice: Stay calm, be brave. Look for signs. What do you think it means?
b. "Make America Great Again." What do you think it means?
c. Hundreds of people of all colors gathered to voice their protests against police brutality against Black Americans. Some carried signs saying, "I can't breathe." What is your interpretation of these events?
d. Between the years 1930 and 1956, Americans were awarded twenty Nobel prizes in medicine. England's doctors received five Nobel prizes during this same period. What is your interpretation of that data?
e. The annual salary of the president of the United States is $400,000. The annual salary of Tom Brady, a football star, is $14,800,000. What is your interpretation of that data?
f. During World War II, the people of Great Britain experienced almost nightly bombing raids by the Nazis. There was a huge loss of life and property. Yet, many people in Great Britain think back about that time with great nostalgia. How do you explain that?
g. Craig continues to get bad marks on his math tests, yet he tries very hard to do well. What explanations can you suggest for that?
h. It wasn't until 1920 that women got the right to vote in America. How do you explain the fact that it took so long for women to be allowed to vote?
i. During Reconstruction, in the American south, there were many incidents of the lynching of Black people. Yet the police did nothing to protect Blacks nor did they arrest the criminals. How do you explain that?
j. When the scientists tested the first atom bomb in New Mexico before the very end of World War II, one of the scientists watching the explosion said, "We have become death." What do you suppose he meant by that?
k. Rick comes to school with clothes that are not clean. He never has his homework. He never finishes his work on time. What can you conclude about this sixth grade boy?

l. Raymondo was crying in the schoolyard. One of the other boys went up to him and asked him what was wrong. Raymondo said, "Leave me alone." How do you explain Raymondo's behavior?

m. More people now use cell phones than landlines. How do you explain it?

n. How do you interpret the behavior of your pet? How can you tell what your pet is trying to tell you?

o. In a famous line from an old comic strip, Pogo said: "We have met the enemy and he is us." What is your interpretation of that statement?

p. Trevor said, "We live in a traditional family." What do you suppose he meant by that?

q. Before the Civil Rights Act made it illegal, Black people in the south had to ride in the rear of the bus, were not allowed to drink water from a fountain marked 'for white people" and couldn't sit at the lunch counter at Woolworth's. How do you explain those rules against Blacks?

r. Justin Bieber? He's famous. What do you think that means?

s. The Simpsons was one of the more popular TV shows. How do you explain its appeal?

t. The Native Americans in New Mexico set up a demonstration to protest against the Columbus Day celebrations. How do you explain their protests?

u. In spite of the alarming rise in cases of COVID-19 across the country, Mr. Gutierrez said, "I won't wear a mask. This is all a hoax." How do you explain Mr. Gutierrez's behavior?

v. "You look like the cat that ate the canary." What does that mean?

w. "Squids are just dumb animals," said Mickey. "It doesn't matter if we cut them up. They don't feel anything anyway." What interpretations has Mickey made about squids?

x. Samantha paid $60 for a pair of designer jeans. She could have had a similar pair, without the designer label, for $30. What explanations can you make about her choice?

y. Kai said it didn't matter if school was closed and he had to stay home for three months. He said he could learn just as much by playing with his apps on his tablet. What explanation can you give for Kai's conclusion?

z. President John F. Kennedy said, "Ask not what your country can do for you. Ask what you can do for your country." What does that statement mean to you?

zz. "How can you trust a person who wears a bow tie?" What does that
statement mean to you?

NOTES TO PARENTS ABOUT
MAKING JUDGMENTS

Criticisms slip from our lips as easily as melting ice in the summer.
We are an army of judges—set out to assess nearly everything we see,
hear, smell, or touch. Those avocados are too ripe; the traffic is a mess;
the clerk at the checkout too slow; the train too crowded; the taxi too
long in coming; the music too loud; the muffin too sweet; the painting
too abstract. Sometimes our judgments are fair and wise; at other times,
they are frivolous, biased, and lacking in "good judgment."

Learning to make good—that is, informed—judgments helps us in a
variety of ways; poor judgments may lead us down the garden path and
into trouble.

Giving children a chance to learn to make better, more informed
judgments enables them to develop a better sense of what has value in
their lives. It helps them to consider, beginning with opinions that are
rooted in information, what is desirable, what is undesirable; what has
beauty, what is ugly; and what has high quality and what is inferior. It
helps them differentiate between what is important and what is trivial.
These are not small benefits. Being able to make choices based on good
judgments is one way to enrich one's life.

One of the downsides of making judgments is when they come from
personal bias, from the desire to inflict pain on others whom we dislike.
That is why it is important when making judgments that they come with
an awareness of how that judgment will impact the lives and well-being
of those being judged. Criticisms are neither wrong or right; they are
more sound when based in good information and less sound when they
are tossed off impulsively.

Learning to judge with compassion and empathy gives us the means
and the tools to become not only more informed but also more considerate and more kind. Especially in these imperiled times, a bit more
kindness of people toward each other cannot be dismissed as not worth
the effort.

These are some of the reasons that making judgments has been
included in the group of higher-order mental operations.

When children have completed an activity from the group below, it is helpful to engage them in a discussion in which not only their judgments are examined but also the means by which they arrived at them. The aim is, once again, to promote further thought about the judgment and especially how that judgment was arrived at.

An example of a parent-child discussion follows:

Parent: You picked the activity that asked for your opinion about the company that dumped toxic waste into the groundwater and children died of leukemia.

Kate: Yeh, I did. Because I had read about that somewhere—I can't remember where and I was so angry to think of the children that died.

Parent: Reading about the incident made you very angry.

Kate: How could the people who were responsible do that stuff. I mean, didn't they care that people and children died? They just dumped the poison into the ground and it leaked into the drinking water.

Parent: There's a lot of anger in your voice when you talk about it.

Kate: Yeh. I don't know what to think about how they should be punished. But they should be punished. The company should be punished.

Parent: You'd like to see the company held responsible for what they did. You want to see them punished.

Kate: Yeh. And I know they got fined for millions of dollars. But that didn't bring the children back.

Parent: You think more needs to be done to punish them.

Kate: Yeh, I don't know what. The money that they were fined is not enough punishment to me.

Parent: You want to see something more. Something more punishing.

Kate: I don't know. I have to think about it.

An Alphabet Soup Plus One of Judging Activities: What's Your Opinion?

In giving your child a task asking for his or her judgment, it is helpful to set up the following guidelines:

- Make sure your judgment comes from information rather than impulsively.
- Make sure your judgment is not angry or hurtful to someone else.
- Make sure your judgment does not show your personal bias in favor of or against a person or thing.

- Use your tablet, your laptop, or your notebook to record your judgments. Make them as clear and as on target as you can.
- Don't be satisfied with a quick, "off the cuff" response. Make sure your judgment is thoughtful and informed.

   a. Mark says he isn't going to wear a face mask. He says he never gets sick.

   b. It doesn't matter if we use plastic bags. They don't take up that much room in the garbage.

   c. Sharona says that Craig's house is a dump because it has no garden.

   d. Patsy says that her teacher is bad because he gives too much homework.

   e. I think we should let all the animals out of the zoo. I think that it's not a happy place to keep animals locked up in cages.

   f. It doesn't matter if we never go back to school. We can learn as much from the Internet.

   g. Kids long ago used to watch Mr. Rogers on TV. I think that kind of program is tired. Very tired.

   h. It doesn't matter who you are. What matters is how much money you have.

   i. People who are mean to dogs and other animals should go to jail. There should be laws against people who hurt animals.

   j. They are going to knock down that whole block of houses in order to build another mall. What are the people going to do about finding another place to live? And who needs another mall?

   k. The government in Brazil is allowing the cutting down of the rain forests—some of the most important natural preserves in the world, in order to make more room for raising cattle.

   l. The chemical company in Massachusetts dumped toxic waste material in the ground. Many children living in that region got leukemia and died. What are your opinions about a company that did this and pretended they didn't do anything wrong?

  m. During the middle of the 1600s, white men went to Africa and captured African men, put them in chains, packed them into the holds of ships, and sailed with them across the Atlantic to the new American colonies. There the Africans were sold as slaves to work on plantations, picking cotton and doing all kinds of hard labor. What kinds of men do you think would do that to other human beings? What is your opinion?

n. When Uncle Ted comes to visit us, he smells of liquor. My mother says I have to hug him but I don't like his smell.

o. I think it's OK to tell a little lie if no one is going to get hurt by it.

p. Priscilla wanted the part of the announcer in the class play. So she lied and told the teacher that she had the right costume. Then she had to go home and tell her mother to buy her the costume.

q. Morelia insists on wearing designer jeans. They cost twice as much as ordinary jeans, which look the same to me.

r. The boys got together and decided to play a trick on Rick, because they didn't like him very much. They said it wasn't mean; it was just fun.

s. I think that spending too much time on your tablet playing with your apps rots your brain.

t. Brian got a gold star for getting all the right answers on his spelling test. But I know he cheated.

u. What are your favorite activities at school? What are your least favorite?

v. What's your favorite movie/TV program/app/book/character in a story?

w. How would you like to see your neighborhood improved?

x. College and professional football are very popular sports. Yet, many players are hurt; some of them hurt badly for all of their lives.

y. Gillie says that some news programs give you fake news, but they are popular nevertheless. And people believe them.

z. There have been many protests by people of all colors against police brutality. Is this a good way to change the way the police behave toward Black people?

zz. Some kids just don't want to think. They just want to be told what to do.

NOTES TO PARENTS ABOUT
SUMMARIZING ACTIVITIES

This is one of the more challenging of the mental operations because the process requires the ability to condense, to distill the "meat" from a body of data. That is, "what is the core message?" To be able to summarize, children must be able to state, briefly and intelligently, the main ideas of something they have read or heard or seen—differentiating between what is important and what may be left out. To do this requires a considerable amount of mental effort, a healthy exercising of the brain.

When children learn to summarize, they become more able to discriminate and to discern relevant from irrelevant, significant from insignificant, consequential from trivial. This enables them to be more understanding of the big ideas of what's really important.

It is possible that some children will have difficulty with this operation, since they are not habituated to discern the "essentials" in a body of data. They are more likely to simply state back what has been seen, or heard or read, recounting it all rather than the "meat." It means they will have to learn to make some decisions about what is to be included and what is to be left out—not an easy task for the beginner.

If that be the case, it may be helpful to give them one or two examples of how this is done, giving them a chance to observe, to analyze the process in which big ideas are extracted from a larger body of information. In some of the activities, where data may be required, children should be free to use any resource, including the Internet, so that they may be more informed about the "whole story."

Before beginning their summary activities, some guidelines can be suggested to smooth the process of inquiry:

- Make some observations about what you have read (seen, heard). Try to figure out what the important message is in those statements.
- What makes you believe that is the important message?
- What parts of the message are less important?
- See if you can summarize the whole of this information in no more than two sentences.

As in the activities above, it is helpful to engage the child in a parent-child discussion to further his or her experience with the process of summarizing. One example of such a discussion is offered here.

An example of a parent-child discussion follows:

Parent: You were working on making a summary of the events that led up to the American Revolution. You seemed to be having a hard time with it.
Randy: I had to look some things up in my textbook. And I also used the Internet.
Parent: You spent some time searching for information that would help you.

Randy: Yeh. I couldn't remember the information from school. I know we studied it. And it had something to do with a tax on tea?
Parent: You weren't sure about the background information. Going to the sources helped you to find out what you needed.
Randy: Yeh. But it didn't help me summarize. I got a lot of information. But making it shorter and figuring out the important parts, that's hard.
Parent: So maybe you need a bit more time to think about how you are going to boil the big story into a small paragraph.
Randy: Yeh. That's hard.
Parent: You want to go back now and keep working on it?
Randy: Yes.
Parent: Can I help you in any way?
Randy: (laughs). Yeh, you can do it for me. But I know you won't do it. I have to do my own thinking.

An Alphabet Soup of Activities that Can be Summarized

a. From your knowledge of the United States (or Canadian) history, write a one-paragraph summary called The Story of the United States (or Canada).
b. Write a one-paragraph summary of your experiences in your class last year.
c. Write a one-paragraph summary of the astronauts' landmark trip to the moon.
d. Write a summary of the procedure you use to change a decimal fraction into a proper fraction.
e. Write a summary of how you divide fractions.
f. Write a two-sentence summary of the last book you read.
g. Write a two-sentence summary of your favorite app.
h. Write a two-sentence summary of how people get infected with the COVID-19 disease.
i. Give a different title to your favorite book.
j. Write a one-paragraph summary of the events leading up to the American Revolution.
k. Write a one-paragraph summary of the events leading up to the American Civil War.
l. Write a one-paragraph summary of what happened to Galileo when he informed the Roman Inquisition that it was the earth that moved around the sun, which was the opposite of what they believed at that time.

m. Write a summary of what happened to Dr. Semmelweis when he was trying to persuade doctors that it was germs that caused infection.

n. Write a short summary of what you know about germs and how they spread disease.

o. Write a short summary of a plan to improve our efforts to clean up our environment.

p. Write a summary of the process in which a caterpillar turns into a butterfly.

q. Write a summary of the invention of the first computer by Alan Turing during World War II.

r. Write a summary of what happened when President Lyndon Johnson signed the Civil Rights Act.

s. Write a summary of the transatlantic slave trade during the sixteenth through nineteenth centuries.

t. Write a summary about the positive and negative effects of immigration.

u. Write a summary of how people learn to become prejudiced.

v. Write a summary of how women got the right to vote in the United States.

w. Write a short summary of the life cycle of salmon.

x. Write a summary of what happens to your garbage after you toss it in the bin.

y. Write a short summary of how IT has influenced your life.

z. Write a short summary of how a person becomes president of the United States.

NOTES TO PARENTS ABOUT DESIGNING PROJECTS AND INVESTIGATIONS

During the few months when the COVID-19 pandemic closed schools and libraries, and children were locked in self-quarantine at home, parents became their teachers, guides, and tutors. In an amazing turn of play, some children freed from the more academic school tasks, turned to invent projects that they carried out with minimal materials—projects that served some intrinsic purpose for them.

For example, Ruby, with a little help from her grandfather, designed a feeding structure for her cat, so that the animal, who had arthritis, would not have to bend over the dish to eat. Barbaraciela created a dramatic project with hand-made puppets, wrote an original play, and built a stage with scenery. She performed the play for her long-distance grandfather on Zoom.

In other words, the projects were not just some time fillers; they addressed certain specific needs. Parents who saw their children so engaged were both amazed and delighted at the creativity they showed. Imagine what satisfaction these children felt as they brought their creative endeavors to fruition.

Designing projects and investigations is the final group of activities for intermediate graders—and the one that encompasses, implicitly, several of the mental operations under its aegis. In these activities, children will have to do some hypothesizing, interpreting, organizing data, and evaluating—but not necessarily in that order.

As any adult already knows, this kind of work begins with a clear appreciation of the nature of the problem to be tackled. Next, one has to figure out what information is needed to move forward to a plan of action. Then, a plan is generated that allows for the creation of the project. (Where materials for the project can be obtained, it is reasonable to expect that children can bring the work to fruition. When materials cannot be obtained, it is of sufficient value to plan the work in a "pencil and paper" design.)

Finally, and perhaps in retrospect, making an appraisal about the methods and the viability of the solution gives an added frisson to the investigative process.

While on the surface, this kind of problem solving seem an accessible task, since many of us engage in that process many times over during our lifetimes, it is not unusual that even adults move to a plan of action FIRST before any of the preceding steps are taken. When that occurs, the solution may be totally disconnected from the problem. That is why working through the suggested stages of designing projects and investigations is a good strategy to enable children to become more skilled and more intelligent problem solvers.

Unlike the other tasks in this section, children may take several days to tackle and complete most of the activities in this group. That is understandable, since they demand more and reach further into the child's capacity to function at this higher level. Obtaining background information from sources, such as newspapers, magazines, and of course, the Internet should be an integral part of these activities.

By way of helping the child gain a foothold on these more challenging tasks, it may be a good idea to set him or her some guidelines for doing the work:

- Begin by stating what you see as the nature of the problem to be tackled. Try to state the problem in a clear and unambiguous way.
- Make some suggestions about where and how you will find the information you need.
- Once you've obtained the information, set out a plan of action that seems reasonable to you.
- If you need to gather materials, make some plans about how to gather them.
- Carry out your plan, either by using the materials to create what you need or with a pencil and paper design.
- Finally, think about the way or ways to figure out how well your plan worked.

Once again, when the child has worked through a design for an investigation, it is helpful to engage in a discussion to determine the strategies used, the procedures, and the effectiveness of the solution.

An example of a parent-child discussion follows:

Parent: You were working on the problem of being the cook for the tree planters. Can you tell me what you did and how you did it?

Josh: That was fun to do. I started by planning to contact the tree planters and find out if any of them had any food preferences and whether any of them had food allergies.

Parent: Wow! I would never have thought of allergies.

Josh: Yeh, because if I stocked up on canned peaches and someone was allergic to peaches, that person would be in trouble.

Parent: So the first thing you planned to do was to find out about food preferences and food allergies.

Josh: Then I would make a list of them. Then I have to figure out what foods would last for the whole time. There would be no refrigerator to keep things cold.

Parent: You'd have to know about the foods that would keep fresh for the whole ten days.

Josh: I'd have to know what month we were talking about because in the hotter months, the foods would spoil quicker. If the weather were colder, there wouldn't be such a problem.

Parent: So you'll need to know more about the time of year and the weather in that area, because keeping the food from going bad would be important.
Josh: Yeh. Then I'd have to figure out something about the quantities. That would be the hardest job.
Parent: Do you have any ideas about how you are going to do that?

A Baker's Dozen Plus One Activities for Designing Projects and Investigations

a. You've been hired as a cook for a group of seventeen tree planters. The eighteen of you are to be flown to Mosquito Lake, a remote area in Wyoming, where you will be engaged in a reforestation project for a period of ten days. There are no access roads to the area and once there, you will have no way of getting out until the plane arrives to take you back. As a cook for the group, you will have to figure out how to feed the seventeen tree planters and yourself in the bush for this ten-day period.

Begin by describing the problem. Then do some research to find out what kind of information you need. Next, develop a plan of action. If you've made any assumptions, it's a good idea to identify them, lest they get in the way of your plan of action. Last, describe what evidence you will use to determine whether your plan was successful.

b. You are on a bicycle trip with a group of five friends, touring central Spain. Your group leader has had bicycle trouble, and she has suggested that you continue on, to the next youth hostel, about twenty-five kilometers away, where she will join you for dinner. However, you have gone much farther than twenty-five kilometers, and you seem to be in the middle of nowhere. There's no cell phone service out here, and it is hard to know what to do. What's more, it's getting dark and there isn't a single person or house to be seen. Suddenly, you come upon this sign: CUIDADO! CAMINO PELIGROSO! PASEAN AL LA DERECHA A CUENCA. 5 km. Only your group leader knows Spanish. What's your plan of action?

Begin by describing the problem. Then, do some research to find out what kind of information you need. Next, develop a plan of action. If you've made any assumptions, it's a good idea to identify them, lest they get in the way of implementing your ideas. Last, describe what evidence you will use to determine whether your plan was successful.

c. You have been asked by the school principal to create a map of the area around your school—identifying important buildings, parks, libraries, and recreational facilities, to give to new students to help them become familiar with the area. The map should be drawn to scale. Before you begin, think about the following:

- What kind of map will it be?
- How will you gather information for your measurements?
- What buildings and other landmarks will you include?
- What materials will you need?
- What scale will you use? How will you do your calculations?

Begin by describing the problem. Then, do some research to find out what kind of information you need. Next, develop a plan of action. If you've made any assumptions, it's a good idea to identify them, lest they get in the way of implementing your ideas. Last, describe what evidence you will use to determine whether your plan was successful.

d. Make a model to show how the human circulatory system functions. As you think about this problem, consider the following:

- What kinds of models might you consider?
- How will you go about choosing the model?
- Where will you find the data you need?
- What scale will you use?

Begin by describing the problem. Then, do some research to find out what kind of information you need. Next, develop a plan of action. If you've made any assumptions, it's a good idea to identify them, lest they get in the way of implementing your ideas. Last, describe what evidence you will use to determine whether your plan was successful.

e. Draw up a plan to help younger children who have been housebound during the self-isolation period of the COVID-19 pandemic. Your plan should include what they can do on their own to educate themselves as well as keep them occupied productively.

Begin by describing the problem. Then, do some research to find out what kind of information you need. Next, develop a plan of action. If you've made any assumptions, it's a good idea to identify them, lest they get in the way of implementing your ideas. Last, describe what evidence you will use to determine whether your plan was successful.

f. Your job is to create a video film that would be entertaining as well as educational for primary grade children.

Begin by describing the problem. Then, do some research to find out what kind of information you need. Next, develop a plan of action. If you've made any assumptions, it's a good idea to identify them, lest they get in the way of implementing your ideas. Last, describe what evidence you will use to determine whether your plan was successful.

g. Develop a plan that would involve children of your own age in taking a stand against racism.

Begin by describing the problem. Then, do some research to find out what kind of information you need. Next, develop a plan of action. If you've made any assumptions, it's a good idea to identify them, lest they get in the way of implementing your ideas. Last, describe what evidence you will use to determine whether your plan was successful.

h. Develop a plan that would disabuse people from believing in UFO's.

Begin by describing the problem. Then, do some research to find out what kind of information you need. Next, develop a plan of action. If you've made any assumptions, it's a good idea to identify them, lest they get in the way of implementing your ideas. Last, describe what evidence you will use to determine whether your plan was successful.

i. Design an app that would help younger children become more fluent readers.

Begin by describing the problem. Then, do some research to find out what kind of information you need. Next, develop a plan of action. If you've made any assumptions, it's a good idea to identify them, lest they get in the way of implementing your ideas. Last, describe what evidence you will use to determine whether your plan was successful.

j. Design some tools that would enable you to measure the speed of sound.

Begin by describing the problem. Then, do some research to find out what kind of information you need. Next, develop a plan of action. If you've made any assumptions, it's a good idea to identify them, lest they get in the way of implementing your ideas. Last, describe what evidence you will use to determine whether your plan was successful.

k. Design a plan of action that would encourage more children to become more considerate of protecting the environment.

Begin by describing the problem. Then, do some research to find out what kind of information you need. Next, develop a plan of action. If you've made any assumptions, it's a good idea to identify them, lest they get in the way of implementing your ideas. Last, describe what evidence you will use to determine whether your plan was successful.

l. You have been chosen as the first child to go to live on the International Space Station, currently in orbit. What preparations do you need to make in order to make your trip and your stay on the station successful?

Begin by describing the problem. Then, do some research to find out what kind of information you need. Next, develop a plan of action. If you've made any assumptions, it's a good idea to identify them, lest they get in the way of implementing your ideas. Last, describe what evidence you will use to determine whether your plan was successful.

m. Amira is a new girl in class. She has come from Syria and is new to our culture and our language. Develop a plan that would involve different members of your class in helping her to bridge the gap between her culture and yours.

Begin by describing the problem. Then, do some research to find out what kind of information you need. Next, develop a plan of action. If you've made any assumptions, it's a good idea to identify them, lest they get in the way of implementing your ideas. Last, describe what evidence you will use to determine whether your plan was successful.

n. Design your own project or investigation. It should be something that is important to you and fulfills a special need. Follow the guidelines that you used for the above activity, for example.

Begin by describing the problem. Then, do some research to find out what kind of information you need. Next, develop a plan of action including the kinds of materials you will need. If you've made any assumptions, it's a good idea to identify them, lest they get in the way of implementing your ideas. Carry out your plans, either on pencil and paper or in a three-dimensional model. Last, describe what evidence you will use to determine whether your plan was successful.

Chapter 7

Endpaper

In this parents' handbook for promoting children's habits of intelligent thinking at home, hundreds of activities have been offered that are rooted in the higher-order thinking operations—mental processes that require children to do some critical thinking. In the author's experiences with "teaching for thinking," none of these activities is beyond the reach of most primary and intermediate graders. In the author's experiences, none of what has been offered is beyond the capabilities of parents who are being called upon to act as tutor, teacher, guide, and helper.

Careful instructions have been laid out for the "how" of getting the most benefit from this work. Examples of how to conduct a parent-child discussion that provokes further thought and taps the kind of thinking that went into the work have been offered in every area. Suggestions for the kinds of questions and responses that bring the best results have been identified as well. In other words, this book not only provides resources for children to use but also serves as a guide to enable parents to do the best kind of teaching that "open minds" in their home contexts.

So why should parents consider taking on this work? What benefits can they expect to see after devoting some time and energy to these activities?

A FEW LAST WORDS

What happens to the children as a result of long-term experiences in higher-order thinking? What are some observable, tangible changes in the behavior of your child that will occur as a consequence of this "teaching for thinking" emphasis?

If past experience and classroom research has any validity it is clear that in the presence of such higher-order thinking experiences, children's behavior will become, noticeably, more thoughtful, and more reflective. They will become less impulsive in drawing conclusions, less dogmatic about a particular point of view, more likely to assume responsibility for their own thinking and more flexible in seeing alternative points of view. None of this happens in a day or a week; but those positive changes do occur over time, after many experiences with these kinds of tasks.

These are the observable signs in behavior that teachers and parents have seen as they have carried out this work with their children. And in an even more surprising result, teachers and parents have noted that children are better able to recall factual information with increasing facility.

If there is one additional benefit that parents may leave with their children to be used throughout their lives, it is hoped that it is the enabling of them as mature, thoughtful, autonomous adults, who are able to face what life has to offer in the increasingly complex worlds of the twenty-first century.

Bibliography

Bloom, Benjamin. 1956. *Taxonomy of Educational Objectives: Cognitive Domain.* New York: David McKay Company.

Kahneman, Daniel. 2011. *Thinking Fast and Slow.* New York: Doubleday.

Index

Anderson, Hans Christian, 36
assumption identification, middle
    graders and, 30, 48; bullies in
    school activity in, 67; clothes
    choosing activity in, 66; critical
    thinking skills in, 65; germs
    activity in, 68; global warming
    activity in, 67; high salary jobs
    activity in, 67; logical reasoning
    in, 18; news bombardment in, 65;
    parent-child discussion example
    for, 65–66; presidential candidate
    activity in, 66; skill development
    in, 65; toothpaste advertisement
    activity in, 67; TORDAN 22K
    activity in, 66; truth and fact in,
    65; women voting rights activity
    in, 67

Barnum, P. T., 65
Bloom, Benjamin, 3
Bridges, Ruby, 58, 59

children. *See specific topics*
classifying, middle graders and:
    alphabet exercise in, 54; book
    list for, 54; diseases list for, 54;
elephant and hippo and giraffe
    exercise in, 53; group purpose in,
    52; human residences list for, 54;
    insects list for, 54; list making
    for, 52; order in, 52; parent-child
    discussion example for, 52–53;
    potatoes and chocolate cake
    exercise in, 53; sea creatures list
    for, 54; TV ads list for, 54; violin
    and drum and flute exercise in, 54
classifying, pre-and emerging readers
    and: animals and, 33; birds and,
    34; children and categories in, 15;
    children and tasks experience in,
    15–16; crayons and, 33; grouping
    purpose in, 33; household tools
    and, 33; musical instruments
    and, 33; order in, 15, 16, 32;
    pre-readers and emerging readers
    in, 33; related groups use in, 15;
    Sonia example of, 32, 33; two
    steps in, 15
cognitive levels, 1–3, 23
comparing, middle graders and:
    advance preparation and asterisk
    use in, 46; doctor and teacher in,
    48; farm and city living in, 48;

90 *Index*

imagining, pre-and emerging readers
and: Anderson and Turing use of,
36; children response to, 37; as
higher-order mental operation, 16;
hot air balloon in, 37; importance
of, 37; inner resource of, 16;
inventions and, 16; invisible
making as, 37; lost in woods as,
37; moon walking as, 37; North
Pole living in, 37; pet chimp in,
37; pig talking in, 37; sea monster
in, 38; Wright brothers and, 36
interpreting, middle graders and, 72;
ability in, 68; American south
and black people exercise in, 70;
atomic bomb testing exercise in,
70; cat ate canary exercise in,
71; Cherokee advice exercise in,
70; conclusion jumping in, 68;
data in, 20; Kennedy exercise
in, 71; meaning in, 20; meaning
missing in, 20; mental operation
requirements in, 20; message
essence in, 20; Native American
Columbus Day protest exercise
in, 71; parent-child discussion
example for, 69–70; pet behavior
exercise in, 71; president and
football player salary exercise in,
70; qualifier use in, 69; right to
vote exercise in, 70; skill gaining
in, 20; traditional family exercise
in, 71; training and lack of, 68;
understanding in, 68–69; World
War II and Great Britain exercise
in, 70

Johnson, Lyndon, 78
judgment making, middle graders
and: African men captured
activity for, 74; animals out of
zoo activity for, 74; Brazil rain

forest cutting activity for, 74;
children and informed judgments
benefits in, 72; compassion
and empathy in, 72; criticisms
and, 72; face mask activity for,
74; favorite movie character
activity for, 75; guidelines for,
73–74; lie telling activity for,
75; neighborhood improvement
activity for, 75; parent-child
discussion example in, 73; people
mean to dogs activity for, 74;
personal bias in, 72; plastic bags
activity for, 74; police brutality
protest activity for, 75; toxic
waste dumping activity for, 74;
trick playing activity for, 75. *See
also* evaluating and judging

Kahneman, Daniel, 3
Kennedy, John F., 71
King, Martin Luther, 48, 57, 59
King, Stephen, 2

material: "higher-order thinking
tasks" use of, 10; observing
use of, 31; thinking operations
availability of, 26
middle graders. *See specific topics*

observing, middle graders and:
accuracy in, 48; animal behavior
activity for, 51; assumption
and opinion avoidance in, 48;
bird nest building activity for,
51; Canada map activity for,
52; crab image activity for, 51;
discussion importance in, 49;
human circulatory system activity
for, 51; Internet data caution in,
49; judgment avoidance in, 49;
musical instrument sound activity

—

About the Author

Selma Wassermann is professor emerita in the Faculty of Education at Simon Fraser University and holder of the University Award for Teaching Excellence. Her books include *Evaluation Without Tears* (2020), *Teaching in the Age of Disinformation* (2018), *What's the Right Thing to Do?* (2019), *Teaching for Thinking Today* (2009), *This Teaching Life* (2004), *The Art of Interactive Teaching* (2017), and *An Introduction to Case Method Teaching: A Guide to the Galaxy* (1994).

Milton Keynes UK
Ingram Content Group UK Ltd.
UKHW011033201123
432908UK00005BA/812